"I've seen Bev completely transform an advisor's practice by giving them a clear and detailed path to follow for sustainable growth. She's an expert marketer and sales coach, and her insights into how humans think, feel and communicate can help anyone be more effective. This handbook should be on every advisor's desk—just commit to doing each step of the plan and you'll see incredible results!"

— *Gail Graham, Chief Marketing Officer*
United Capital Financial Advisors

More Advance Praise for
The Pocket Guide to Sales for Financial Advisors

"Over the next three to five years, the most client-focused members of the advisory profession are going to have to become far more professional in their marketing activities. I predict that *The Pocket Guide to Sales* will be instrumental in that important transition."

— Bob Verres, Inside Information
Insider's Forum Conference

"This 'little' book is packed with so many good ideas from strategic to tactical. I highly recommend it to any financial advisor who needs a business-building boost."

— Eric Godes, COO & Chief Wealth Advisory Officer
Federal Street Advisors

"Clear, concise, executable... Beverly Flaxington distills the essences of the sales workflow. Case studies crystalize the points in each chapter. You will understand why you need to build a sales culture and how to do it. Why effective storytelling is necessary and how to construct one. We all have more work than time. This book shows you how to focus your time and efforts on business building. A must-have guide to grow your business!"

— Mary Ann Buchanan, CEO & Founder
RIA Match

Beverly D. Flaxington

The Pocket Guide to Sales for Financial Advisors

Published by ATA Press

ISBN: 978-0-9837620-8-9

Library of Congress Control Number: 2014953404

First printing: November, 2014

Table of Contents

I have had the distinct pleasure of working one-on-one with hundreds of advisors over the years. Know that I dedicate this book to all of you — what you allowed me to teach and what you helped me to learn from our interactions.

Thank you and sell on!

Foreword

As a financial advisor, does it feel uncomfortable to think of yourself as a salesperson? If so, you are not alone. Most CFPs®, CFAs®, and financial advisors feel this way. As professionals, we want to help people, not sell people!

Maybe we feel this way because there are many negative associations to the word. For many, it conjures up images of being pushy and influencing people to do things they don't want to do. However, if you want to effectively grow your business and help more people, sharing who you are and how you can help is critical. Guess what? That skill is called selling, and the sales component of your business is essential to your success. The good news is that it can and absolutely should be approached in a thoughtful way. By doing so, you will effectively influence your prospects and clients while growing your business.

This is where *The Pocket Guide to Sales* comes in. In this book, Beverly Flaxington brings over 25 years of experience as a consultant and coach to hundreds of advisors in our industry, and guides you to improve your practice from a sales perspective. This guide truly covers every aspect you need to be comfortable, effective, and successful.

Whether you are just starting your career as a financial advisor or you are seasoned and wish to strategically grow your practice, this book will serve as your trusted guide. In the following pages you will find a comprehensive sales manual, a workbook that leads you step-by-step to create your unique sales plan, and a supportive coach who provides gentle encouragement to embrace sales, help more people, and grow your business. You will move from feeling uncomfortable about sales to developing confidence and exceeding your goals.

Sheri Smith
VP of Sales & Lead Generation, United Capital

Introduction

Selling is as old as civilization itself. Put in the simplest of terms, selling is the exchange of goods and services for something of value.

To financial advisors, however, the sale is often seen in a negative light, and many cringe at the word "sell." Interestingly, the same advisors who shy away from the concept of selling are often those who find themselves selling every single day! Sometimes they're even participating in the selling process multiple times throughout the day—and they may not realize it. Asking for client referrals, developing strategic alliances, seeking and talking with new prospects are all obvious parts of the selling process, but selling happens every time you remind a client why it's a good choice to do business with you, too.

The fact is that most CFAs®, CFPs®, CPAs, and other professionals did not obtain these titles because deep down they really wanted to be in sales. Most times, their interests tend more toward data, analysis, and more solitary orientations. Selling is probably the last thing those who entered these fields were thinking of doing. They may not have considered the "people" aspect of their chosen profession; the aspect that involves sales.

For this reason, and some others, turning into a salesperson seems like a negative, degrading thing. Many advisors will conjure up the picture of the slimy used-car sales guy. It's time to recognize selling as the valuable activity that it is. It is a way to:

- Let people know who you are and what you do well.
- Get your message out to those who need it.
- Promote your planning process, wealth management services, or investment expertise.
- Use your relationship skills to close new business.
- Take your business to the next level.

If you want to grow your business, the bottom line is that you — or someone on your team — need to sell, and to sell well. This book will offer guidance on how you can sell in a comfortable and effective manner.

Fig. 2.

SECTION I:
Improving Your Practice from a Sales Perspective

CHAPTER I

Diagnosis: The Sales Effectiveness Model

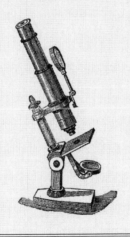

"*As you travel down life's highway... whatever be your goal, you cannot sell a doughnut without acknowledging the hole.*"

—Harold J. Shayler

There are lots of elements to selling, and this book will attempt to cover many of them. The first place for any financial advisor to start is by looking at their practice. It's always important to start with diagnosing what's not working, and then asking why effective selling isn't as easy as it could be.

Unfortunately, in many cases, the advisor doesn't know what's really wrong and why they don't sell or close as much as they'd like. They might believe coaching for their advisors is the answer, or hiring a "hunter," or increasing the compensation for new business will make a difference. Just as you would not construct a portfolio for a new high net worth client without understanding their situation, first you need to spend time in uncovering what's working and what's not in your practice before you can develop an answer to the problem.

Rather than trying to fix things that aren't going to make a difference, first focus on those areas that are the current pain points. A good portfolio involves selecting individual components to make up the overall diversification for the client. Similarly, for any one individual or financial advisory firm to be successful in sales, the basic building blocks must be in the right places. And just like you would have a business plan for your overall financial advisory practice, with goals and objectives and milestones, an effective sales process includes preparing a business development plan and a sales strategy to mirror that plan.

The Sales Effectiveness Model©, developed by our firm,

has been used with hundreds of advisors, both small and large, and is a method used to help uncover any weaknesses that might be hindering sales. These eight factors are the basic keys to sales success. Before you try and increase your personal sales skill level, take a look at your firm overall.

Once you are clear about what you need to focus on, the rest of the book will provide the answers you need to become more sales savvy and effective.

Diagram 1: The Sales Effectiveness Model

Sales Effectiveness Model

The proprietary Sales Effectiveness Model incorporates eight key factors which are critical to the sales and marketing success of any firm. Using this model, first assess where obstacles to sales success are evident. Then prioritize actions in the highest-need areas and, finally, implement a plan for resolving these obstacles to ensure success.

1. Define Markets and Offerings: Passing the "So What?" Test

Begin at the beginning. Before you define a sales strategy or attempt to redefine one that isn't working, your offerings must have a clearly defined target market and provide clear solutions for that market. Your firm must understand the market it is pursuing, why the offerings are unique, and the compelling competitive positioning. Defining your market and brand provides a platform from which your team can sell more effectively; without a strong brand, there is no story to be told.

2. Sales Strategy: Leveraging all Available Avenues, Including Selling to Existing Clients

After a marketing strategy is defined, sales strategy—how you will find the prospects for your financial advisory practice—is the next most important component. Problems in the day-to-day prospecting and selling process often arise because of lack of vision and focus on strategy. For advisors, the most common sales channels are Centers of Influence or strategic alliances, existing clients (referrals), direct marketing (via mail or email), networking events, or direct selling.

3. Sales Talent: Identifying the "Right" Talent

It's critical that anyone in a sales capacity fit the role and the firm culture. The competition for talent is fierce today, so it's critical to identify "A" players during the hiring process and then, once hired, continue to motivate and excite those players to stay on your team. Minimizing turnover and avoiding the process of churning people through a company needs to be a key focus of any successful sales effort.

4. Sales Skills

The hallmark of effective sales is the ability to master a wide diversity of skills. Several of these focus on the often underemphasized and underdeveloped qualifying skill, which is really about managing time and optimizing it for success. Identifying the skills your advisors have, or may be lacking, and coaching or managing to those skills is a must.

5. Sales Compensation

Many financial advisors do not align their sales compensation with their business objectives. Instead, they create two plans in a vacuum without considering, or even being aware of, the consequences of this mismatch. Compensation programs must be motivating, but also must support the firm's overall objectives in order to be effective and useful.

6. Sales Support

You may have great-looking marketing materials and a slick web site, but to ensure the most effective use by those delivering your message, marketing communications must align with your sales process. Most firms waste time and money on materials that are never used, or are used ineffectively.

7. Leveraging Technology (CRM)

Prospecting, pipeline creation, reporting, and the integration of other business functions are critical to managing the sales process. These tools need to be in place and working smoothly to optimize the effectiveness of your efforts. In addition to identifying the best tools for your organization, the firm needs to train and support utilization of the tools for ongoing success.

8. Effective Internal Communication

The information required for effective selling and presenting the right image about your firm to the marketplace must be readily available. Critical information must be obtained about prospects and the market, and then a feedback process must be in place to build relationships, get the team motivated, and create a sales culture.

Activity: Sales Effectiveness Evaluation Checklist

When you are ready to perform a thorough assessment on your own, here is an extensive list of the questions to be asked using the Sales Effectiveness Model. Once you have identified the areas of weakness, you will find answers throughout the book on how to solve these for your practice.

Factor 1. Define Market & Product Offerings

☐ Are you clear about who are your "best" prospects and clients? Can you define a clear profile of the best fit for your firm?

☐ Do you know which clients haven't been a fit and why? Are there trends you can identify?

☐ Do you know how to locate the right target prospects—where are they and how do you reach them?

☐ Do you know the scope of your market? How many target prospects do you have?

☐ Are you clear on your competitors? Can you articulate the differences between your offerings and those of the competition?

☐ Have you defined the products and services you offer, and the problems of the target market they solve?

☐ Do you have a compelling and differentiating story about your firm, your services, and yourself?

Factor 2: Sales Channels

- [ ] Have you identified, and are you using, other channels to access your target market?
- [ ] Do you know the most effective sales approach for your financial products and services?
- [ ] Are your clients primary referral sources for you?
- [ ] Do you have other reliable and successful referral sources in place?
- [ ] Do you know what the referral sources "need" from you?
- [ ] Have you explored whether there other avenues of distribution?
- [ ] Do you have an infrastructure of support for the different distribution channels?
- [ ] Do you know the primary differences between client referrals, COI referrals, or other channels—and their different requirements?

Factor 3: Sales Talent

- [ ] Do you know the profile of a "top performing" business developer for your firm?
- [ ] Can you articulate the cultural fit of a salesperson—what should they value and how should they work with others to fit in your firm?
- [ ] Have you outlined clearly and in writing specific expectations for people in a sales capacity?
- [ ] Do you know the kind of background

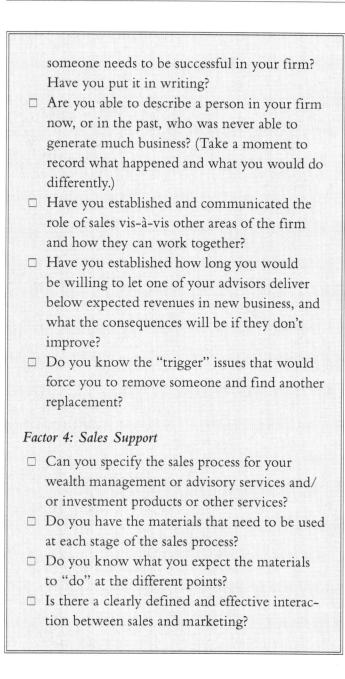

someone needs to be successful in your firm? Have you put it in writing?

☐ Are you able to describe a person in your firm now, or in the past, who was never able to generate much business? (Take a moment to record what happened and what you would do differently.)

☐ Have you established and communicated the role of sales vis-à-vis other areas of the firm and how they can work together?

☐ Have you established how long you would be willing to let one of your advisors deliver below expected revenues in new business, and what the consequences will be if they don't improve?

☐ Do you know the "trigger" issues that would force you to remove someone and find another replacement?

Factor 4: Sales Support

☐ Can you specify the sales process for your wealth management or advisory services and/ or investment products or other services?

☐ Do you have the materials that need to be used at each stage of the sales process?

☐ Do you know what you expect the materials to "do" at the different points?

☐ Is there a clearly defined and effective interaction between sales and marketing?

☐ Is new business information passed readily and easily between the different areas in your practice?

☐ Are your advisors trained to sell?

☐ Do you know for each of them, including your own selling skills, what has worked and what hasn't?

☐ Do your service and administrative staff understand that non-sales people are also performing a sales role?

Factor 5: Sales Compensation

☐ Do you outline the expected revenue goals on an annual basis?

☐ Do you define and communicate overall new business expectations and the sources that you expect for revenue?

☐ Do you know where you fall in terms of compensation vis-à-vis your competition?

☐ Does your compensation program allow for "other than sales" activities, such as canvassing the market for market feedback or product enhancements?

☐ Is your sales plan consistent with your business plan?

☐ Are advisors motivated in alignment with the overall business strategy?

Factor 6: Technology

☐ Do your employees have electronic capability when they travel?

☐ Are they fully supported on the road?

☐ Do you have a sales contact management system?

☐ Do you have clearly defined requirements to put in information?

☐ Can you use the information once the prospect becomes a client?

☐ If you don't have a contact management system, do you have an alternative system to track prospects and pipeline?

☐ Are there reports that you, and other management, wish you had?

☐ Do you know what kind of information you are missing?

☐ Do you have adequate prospecting lists available on the system with easy accessibility?

Factor 7: Qualification

☐ Are you clear about the steps from first contact to close for most prospects?

☐ Do you regularly do post-mortems to understand who becomes a client and why, and who does not?

☐ Can you or your staff clearly articulate the needs of each and every prospect they are talking with?

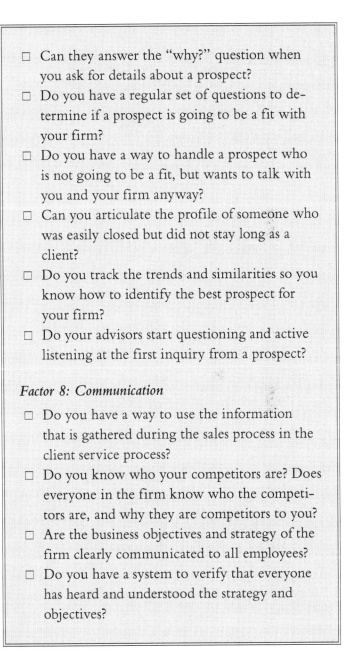

- ☐ Can they answer the "why?" question when you ask for details about a prospect?
- ☐ Do you have a regular set of questions to determine if a prospect is going to be a fit with your firm?
- ☐ Do you have a way to handle a prospect who is not going to be a fit, but wants to talk with you and your firm anyway?
- ☐ Can you articulate the profile of someone who was easily closed but did not stay long as a client?
- ☐ Do you track the trends and similarities so you know how to identify the best prospect for your firm?
- ☐ Do your advisors start questioning and active listening at the first inquiry from a prospect?

Factor 8: Communication

- ☐ Do you have a way to use the information that is gathered during the sales process in the client service process?
- ☐ Do you know who your competitors are? Does everyone in the firm know who the competitors are, and why they are competitors to you?
- ☐ Are the business objectives and strategy of the firm clearly communicated to all employees?
- ☐ Do you have a system to verify that everyone has heard and understood the strategy and objectives?

☐ Do you have sales meetings and regularly communicate themes on what's working and what's not to any client-facing employees?

☐ Do you seek to understand and then fix communication flaws that most people in your practice raise?

While not an exhaustive list, these are common areas that advisory firms have often not addressed, or are pain points hampering the new business development process. Review these areas and check those that are working and in place. Focus on those that you are not able to check as you continue through the book.

CHAPTER II

Standing Out in a Crowded Market: Brand Effectiveness

"*Your brand is a gateway to your true work. You know you are here to do something — to create something or help others in some way. The question is, how can you set up your life and work so that you can do it? The answer lies in your brand. When you create a compelling brand, you attract people who want the promise of your brand — which you deliver.*"

—Dave Buck

The Sales Effectiveness Model starts with a definition of your market and offerings, and a knowledge of your brand. Without a brand platform and clear direction about what you are selling and to whom, the sales process cannot be sustainable and effective over the long term. Investopedia describes a brand as "A distinguishing symbol, mark, logo, name, word, sentence or a combination of these items that companies use to distinguish their product from others in the market."[1]

But a brand is much more than this in the selling process. When done well, it provides a foundational platform from which to launch a strong business development process and create consistent and compelling materials, and from which to tell stories about what you do and how you do it. Every firm and individual practice needs a brand as well as the positioning in the market and the value proposition (what you do well and differently) that accompanies it.

Financial advisors know that many other similar firms say the exact same thing they do when talking about their value proposition. "We are independent and objective" can refer to nearly every registered independent advisor in the market. With over 40% of financial advisors over 55 years old, "We have longevity and tenure" applies to most! Commonly, financial advisors will say things like the following to "differentiate" themselves:

- We have a process (for investment, client engagement, portfolio construction, etc.).

1   *Investopedia* (Website), s.v. "Brand," accessed August 12, 2014, http://www.investopedia.com/terms/b/brand.asp.

- We communicate with our clients.
- We "partner" with our clients.
- Our performance is solid.
- We have experience, tenure, and well-qualified people.
- We listen to our clients.
- We focus on our clients' needs and create customized answers.

All of these statements are very positive, and all financial advisors can probably own them and use them; unfortunately, they are too common. The problem is, from a branding perspective, these are basic things that don't really differentiate one advisor from another advisor.

It's important to think from the investor's perspective—the person listening to you in the sales process. Why should they care about any of these common statements? For example, what does it do for them that you communicate with your clients? How does partnering with them provide value? It's important to make the connection about what you are saying and why they should care about it. With any marketing platform, it's important to answer the "So what?" question—so what is important about this statement to me?

That is where branding comes in.

Branding

A building block of a successful marketing campaign is branding. It is important to discover your brand, figure out how it is perceived by your audience, and determine how it can add value to your business and your clients. A brand is not just a logo. It's not a catchy phrase, or a product. It is the sum total of the experience and perception of you by your current and prospective clients. Most importantly, your brand should define you, it should be recognized, and it should be different from that of your competitors.

Talking about what you do and why it's different should ultimately translate into your firm's "story." The platform, or brand, is why you are different, and the platform points show where you are different—and how.

It's vital to a successful business-building effort to stay consistent with your brand and to weave the brand points through all of your communications. When this is done properly and well, prospects and clients will remember what's different about your firm.

Steps for Developing Brand

- Create a list of what you do well and differently—get team members involved in this process.
- Once you have the list of those things you think are special or different, put your differentiators to the "so what?" test. Next to what you've written, ask "so

what?" Why is this important or compelling for your audience?

- Review your mission statement or firm values to find the words you use to talk about what's important to your practice. If you haven't written a mission statement or identified firm values, it's helpful to do that during a branding process.

- Interview clients and Centers of Influence (COIs) to learn how they talk about what you do. Don't do a satisfaction survey; rather, interview them to hear the words they use to describe their experience of working with you. See your firm through their lens.

- Review your competition to understand their themes and differentiators.

- While you may want to focus on a number of things, force your team to choose the three themes or differentiators that your competitors are not using, and meet the "so what?" test.

- Find ways to validate those three differentiators and create proof statements and stories to support them.

- Weave the points into all of your marketing communication efforts—be consistent with these points throughout all of your materials and sales process.

While you may believe the wealth management and advisory services you offer are unique and special, the market may not feel the same. To be competitive, you must know your own services better than your competitors know their own, and you must know the benefits of your services from the client's perspective. How do clients talk about what you do and why it is special?

People don't buy services or products. They buy what the product or service will do for them. They buy benefits. They buy solutions to problems and satisfaction of their wants and needs. They are not hiring "just" a financial planner; they are hiring someone to take a weight off their shoulders, help them navigate difficult circumstances, and take care of them!

 Case Story

One advisory firm wanted to stand out in a crowded retirement plan servicing market. They had a number of competitors close by who were doing similar things. They went through the following process:

1. Listed the things they believed were different about their firm and approach.
2. Asked the "so what?" question for each differentiator to identify what mattered and why to their audience.
3. Reviewed their competition to see what they were saying about what they did and how they did it.
4. Interviewed their retirement clients to ask what words they used to describe what they did.
5. Pulled out the three themes they believed were most different, and could be supported by facts and experience.

They ultimately determined their brand to be "The Accessible Retirement Experts" and concluded that their platform points were depth of knowledge, willingness to customize, and legal expertise.

While these three points are not extremely different as stand-alone components, their relevance to what their competitors were saying, combined with the way the firm tells its story, allows them to come alive in a memorable way for prospects and clients.

CHAPTER III

The Power of Niche Marketing: Finding Your Natural Niche

"Identify your niche and dominate it. And when I say dominate, I just mean work harder than anyone else could possibly work at it."

—Nate Parker

The best sales materials are those that speak to your audience. As adult learners, we connect most quickly when the message resonates with something we recognize and care about. This truism illustrates the power of niche marketing. A niche is some portion of the market that shares a special characteristic—demographic, lifestyle, interests, background, buying behavior, etc. A niche makes it possible for small businesses to carve out a segment of the marketplace, define their strengths, and focus on those, instead of trying to make a broad appeal. Knowing your brand, as discussed in the previous chapter, is the "what we do and why it is so important"—having a niche market says "who we do this for most effectively." One of the fastest ways to gain recognition is to find your niche, focus on your niche, and do excellent work within that niche.

Occupying a niche means you'll be offering your financial planning or wealth management services to a specific and select group of people. Many advisors question the relevance of a niche and worry that it will pigeonhole their efforts. The planning process, for example, could work for everyone from the single corporate executive to the multi-family office. The power of having a niche is that it gives the advisory firm focus and allows for marketing efforts to have a sharp, natural focus.

Finding your niche begins with doing some internal and external investigation. Analyze your best clients and determine any themes or common characteristics. Identify the characteristics of those prospects who need what you do and can understand your value to them. Descriptors can be anything—as detailed as doctors in private practice who are planning for retirement to more broad such as divorced women. Knowing the niche market's needs helps you develop a message that resonates with them.

You may not think in terms of niche now, but likely there are natural niches within your current client base.

Target Markets

Simply saying "All investors over $250,000" or "All investors over $1 million" is going to make your new business development efforts much harder, because the descriptors are so broad. Being broad sounds better—lots more opportunity—but in reality, when you define a niche and become known by that niche you can speak to them with a message created around their specific needs.

There are endless ways to create a message and strategy for the segments on which you want to focus. The fastest way to stand out in a crowded market is to take a message into the market that is clear, crisp, and different, yet understandable to a targeted segment. The way the human brain works, and the manner by which adults learn new information, is that they hear those statements or ideas that really resonate with them. They'll tend to throw out anything that doesn't fit their understanding of who they are.

This means—from a target market perspective—that speaking the lingo of the groups you are targeting is key to reaching them. If they hear words and jargon that resonate with them, they'll listen. Likewise, if they believe you really understand their specific needs and issues, they'll be more apt to open up to you.

It is not necessary to select just one specific market and pursue it without regard to other opportunities. Pick a few segments that you've either been successful in historically, that you have some existing knowledge about, or that you think would be a particularly good fit for your offerings.

One advisor was adamant that his work was too broad and necessary for everyone. He didn't believe in a natural niche, and didn't think one existed in his client base. Once he reviewed his clients in some detail, looking at his "ideal" clients and his best clients, he found an interesting theme: Several of them had a background as engineers who had decided to pursue new careers. He began to message differently, speaking to engineers and ex-engineers about how his investment process fit their mindset and way of thinking. He was able to put together materials and workshops that spoke to anyone who was, or had once been, an engineer. The referrals started to increase amongst this niche. After a year of focusing on this niche, he was asked to speak to a large company of engineers, and he became involved with their HR department to offer financial workshops directly to engineering, and other, employees.

To consider what natural niches you might have in your client base, ask yourself and your team the following:

- Who are our ideal or best clients? How do we describe them?
- How did our best clients come to us?
- What problems or needs do they have when they come to us?
- What do we know about our clients? For example, what are their hobbies, interests, backgrounds, associations, etc.?
- How could we segment our clients—by theme?
- How do we solve client problems? What do we do for them to solve problems?

You probably believe you know your clients very well, and you probably do know aspects about them. To find a niche market, you want to start looking at them in a different way. Who are they? What are their interests?

Case Story

One client we had knew his clients very well; they'd been working together for 25 years. He wanted to do more targeted niche marketing in order to increase client referrals. He started to look at his client base and dig down for hobbies, interests, and places they liked to go. He found he had a theme of wealthy people who played tennis. They didn't belong to the same club, but they all enjoyed the sport and played every time they could. Instead of marketing "We work with wealthy tennis players," he started to incorporate tennis themes into his marketing, and held events at tennis-related venues. Because the clients were drawn to this, they brought their wealthy tennis-playing friends. He began to build the business focused on this niche.

This is the beauty of niche marketing; once you have the niche, you can do a variety of things to appeal to what they like and care about.

CHAPTER IV
Marketing Strategy and Tactics

"Marketing is too important to be left to the marketing department."

—David Packard

Marketing is a process of developing and putting into practice a plan which identifies, anticipates, and satisfies client requirements in such a way that a profit is realized. Market research and planning appropriate marketing methods are important parts of marketing.

The two requirements for successful marketing of any practice are to have both a marketing strategy and a marketing plan. These go hand in hand and are often confused. A marketing strategy is a list of the goals to attain as a result of marketing efforts. The strategy used will depend upon the business goals. The marketing plan is simply how those business goals will be reached. A simple way to remember the difference between the two is:

Strategy = Thinking
Planning = Doing

Strengths, Weaknesses, Opportunities, & Threats

Many firms will start by completing an analysis of strengths, weaknesses, opportunities, and threats (SWOT). SWOT is a basic component of any business management program and is relevant to financial advisors, as well.

The first two sections, strengths and weaknesses, represent an internal look at your firm. What are you doing well? What things would you like to keep in place and build upon? What areas would you like to improve? Where, as a firm, do you run into obstacles and get sidetracked from your goals? This is an excellent chance to involve members of your staff and team. Oftentimes people in different roles and with different areas of focus will all see, from their respective vantage point, some of the same issues. This can help the firm to understand where the "real" weaknesses are. Poll your team and find out generally where there is agreement and where there is disagreement about what the firm is doing well and where it needs to improve. Document the results and keep the strengths in mind to build on, while remaining aware of the areas that need improvement.

After you've done the internal look, turn to the external side of the equation—the opportunities and threats. Those are the external aspects that affect your firm. What's happening in the market right now? Who are your main competitors? What market changes, cultural changes, demographic changes, and so on are expected to take place? How will they either open new doors for your firm or close existing ones?

Break Down Your Goals

Once you have the mission and the values very clearly defined, the next step involves breaking down your goals into discrete areas of growth.

The best plans involve clearly defining the areas of focus and defining—as specifically as you are able—what the actual goals look like in a number of different categories. For example, if you want to increase client referrals, you would start by identifying where you are today, and then identify what success looks like for increasing these referrals. This can be by number of new referrals, or by assets under management, or by revenue. By stating a specific goal for each area, you'll be able to measure your success toward that goal and make mid-course corrections when you find you're heading off-track in any one area. It also allows for the allocation of resources and focus, instead of just throwing budget money at something but not knowing how much each segment of your plan should get as an allocation.

Ultimately, you should have identified the different areas within which you hope to improve your business development efforts, and focus your marketing strategy in those areas. So if you are hoping to penetrate the custodial channel and want to increase sales through your relationship there, don't spend a lot of time writing articles for journals in a niche market the custodial reps don't read! Where you want to go should be clear and concise, and then should dictate what marketing tactics you want to apply against your efforts.

Define Sales Channels

A sales channel is how services or products are brought to market for purchase by consumers. A direct sales channel applies if a business sells directly to clients. If a third party is involved in the sale, then it is considered to be an indirect sales channel.

Activity: Documenting Your Sales Process

Take a minute now and outline your sales process. What steps will you and your advisors, or business developers, take from start to close with a new prospect?

Once you have outlined the process, you will want to identify what materials align with each step in the process. What do you use, where do you use it, and what is the purpose of the marketing piece?

It's important to ensure that the materials you have are those you use at each step of the process. Identify any steps you currently take where you don't have materials and flag them as areas for development. See the the next page for an example of this process in action.

The sales channel you choose will affect the marketing methods you use. It's best to decide whether you are selling directly or indirectly to your target market. Most financial advisors sell directly to their clients but are also often using Centers of Influence, branch reps, existing clients, or networking in the community to reach their audience.

#	Activity	Materials Needed
1	Identify a prospect in the CRM system that fits our targeted profile	None
2	Send a letter of introduction about our firm and offerings	Standard introduction letter and one pager on our firm
3	Follow up with a phone call and invite the prospect into our office	Standard pitch book
4	Perform an intake session at the first in-person meeting and learn more about the prospect	Interactive intake form
5	Schedule a second meeting to re-view their portfolio and talk about potential steps we would take to reallocate	One pagers on the planning process and investment approach
6	Send a follow-up letter outlining the steps and any observations	Customized follow-up letter
7	Confirm, via a telephone call, that they are ready to engage as a client	None
8	Send a contract for signature	Contract
9	Begin to work with the client	Welcome package

Diagram 2: Sample Sales Process Documentation

So it is a combination of indirect—through someone else to reach the prospect—and direct, when you sit down with the prospect to talk about your services.

Develop Materials that Make the Audience Care

As you create your marketing plan, you'll need to determine which marketing materials to use at each step in the selling process. It is important to know what you want the materials to accomplish and the purpose you want them to serve.

While they are important as supporting tools, marketing materials alone rarely sell anything— especially something as important as wealth management. Therefore, be careful and specific about what you need and why, and do not waste a lot of time and money putting all of your messaging into written materials. Materials should entice and engage, but they cannot tell the whole story.

There are a few core marketing pieces every advisor should have:

- Updated and search-engine-optimized website
- Standard introductory pitch book
- Brochure or nice "leave behind" giving an overview of the firm and services (your credibility statement)
- One pagers on different capabilities (bios, investment process, the client experience, etc.)
- Direct mail pieces (if this is one of the marketing strategies)
- Newsletter
- Niche-focused pieces

Let's look at one marketing tool that every advisor should

have: the pitch book. Even if you believe you don't need a pitch book, or would not use it, it's important to have because it helps your entire team know the flow and substance of your story, and have a consistent way to tell it.

The Pitch Book: Best Practices

A pitch book is simply a presentation to qualify a prospect and to inform them about what you do and how you do it. It details the most important attributes of your firm. A pitch book is not something to be used as a "mailer" or a "leave behind." It is an active document, and it is meant to be used interactively. During a presentation, it's important to use the pitch book to stay engaged and to learn about and address the questions and concerns of your prospective client. Instead of just delivering content, it is used to create a back-and-forth exchange. The pitch book is useful as a guide to keep the conversation on track, as a tool for the prospect to write down key ideas, and as a leave behind once the meeting is completed to jog further questions or ideas from the prospect.

The pitch book should be very light on words, and is not meant to stand alone. When developing a pitch book, keep in mind the six keys of confident presenting to ensure highest impact in delivery:

1. Know Why: Keys to Content
What is the purpose of the pitch book? What do you want

it to do? Will it be used to educate a potential client? Will it be used as a sales tool? Is it simply an introduction to your firm? If your pitch book is to be utilized as a sales tool, remember not to overload it with too much data; keep it light so you can carry on a conversation, and leave your prospective client wanting to learn more. If, on the other hand, your pitch book is an educational tool, then you'll want to aim at providing data to support your points, use additional handouts so the pitch book isn't overloaded with information and leave time at the end of each section for a question and answer period so you can be sure the audience understands your points. Also, make sure to provide information for different knowledge levels. This will help to keep everyone interested and engaged.

2. Know Who

Understand them. Who is your audience? What do you know about them? No matter whether you're meeting with someone for the first time or if you've had a long-term relationship, you should always have the name of the person or group on the front cover, if possible, and make sure their name is in larger print than yours! Allow one or two pages of information for each topic to promote interactive discussions. Insert questions, if needed. Provide general background information about the types of people with whom you work. Be sure to ask them questions, such as why they are considering using a financial advisor at this time and what their past experiences have been. Use the early portion of the pitch book for questions and probing, so you are sure to find out what is important to them.

3. Create Flow: Chunk it

Outline what you want to tell them, then chunk it down into sections so the prospective client can follow along. Look at your information and create chunks of information in sections, such as:

- A focus on you, the client
- Our firm's philosophy
- The client experience
- The investment process
- What makes us different

The above are only examples. No matter what information is included or how it is set into sections, it is important to provide section headers to separate each discrete "chunk" of information. Make sure to include no more than three or four major points in each section, and don't include anything too complicated. Keep it simple.

4. Create Context

Use case stories and examples so that your audience can relate. Try to have a couple of placeholders in each section to talk about how your philosophy, investment process, etc., helped someone. Develop scenarios of the types of people you work with; if you know enough about your audience in advance, include stories relevant to their life and situation. Always have a section on client experience; tell them what it was like for other clients who have worked with you. If possible, lay this out in a step-by-step manner so they know exactly what to expect.

5. Remember Adult Learning Preferences

Have information presented in a few different ways: pictures, words, stories, etc. Think about where you might insert a picture instead of words to convey an idea, or whether you can arrange information a little differently so it is more pleasing to the eye. Is there information you can put in separate pages, or handouts, so that you can move from the pitch book at times to other information? Adult learners take in things differently—some are visual, some kinesthetic, etc., so deliver the information in a variety of ways. Always stay "light" on words wherever possible.

6. Have a Close: Wrapping it Up

Instead of just ending once you get to the last page, recap for the audience the goals of your presentation. Be sure to identify what you expect them to do next. Perhaps they need to take a next step, or sign on the dotted line. Whatever it is, it is up to you to tell them. You started by identifying the goal of the meeting, now recap what the goal was and establish the next steps. Don't leave it to chance; let them know what you expect. Leave a section for a discussion of next steps and a page for questions. Always end with your contact information.

It's important, also, to remember to put complicated information at the back of your presentation (i.e., data and comprehensive graphs, investment numbers, sample portfolios, additional case stories, etc.).

Review What You Have Now

Review your current materials. Make sure you are talking about the client and their needs. Instead of "We do this and we do that," talk about who you help and why it's important. Remember that people who come from outside the financial services industry are often daunted by the jargon and the perceived complexity. Don't make it worse with your materials! More is not more when it comes to marketing. Be succinct and clear, and remember to always include the context—so what about what you do and why it is important, useful, or helpful to them?

What can be done to make your story come alive? Here are five key points to telling your story in a way that makes the audience care:

1. Step into their shoes.

It may well be true that yours is the greatest firm ever, but you should let the person reading your presentation come to that conclusion. Instead of trying to win the prospect over by telling them about your greatness, tell your story in a way that makes the prospective client say "Aha, this firm is great!" Using subtle messages about what you do and how well you do it works much better. The best messages, though, are those geared to what the audience really cares about—not about what your firm cares about.

2. Less is more.

Cut back on the number of words used and the various themes you are trying to get across. If the prospect or client wants more, have available supporting documentation to give further details. Don't overwhelm them with data and information right up front.

3. Allow time to interact.

When presenting with a pitch book or in person, don't have a complete "data dump" approach. Work in ways to ask the prospective client what they are thinking and understanding, and what they want to know more about. In written materials, consider offering less information so the prospect has to call you to ask questions.

4. Be clear about what you are truly trying to accomplish with marketing material.

What's the purpose of the material? What does "success" look like to the reader when they finish reading? Tailor the information for the purpose intended. Don't use the same approach and materials for all situations. The core messaging should stay the same, but tailor how you incorporate those messages to each situation.

5. Have the call to action clearly stated.

What do you want the audience to do with the information? What's the next step? How should they think/feel or act when they finish reading your materials? Make it clear what they need to do to work with you.

Some Tactics to Consider

The importance of planning simply cannot be underestimated. The firms that take the time to do this find they are able to accomplish much more with fewer people in less time. Today, "doing more with less" is a mantra for many firms.

Let's look at some possible marketing tactics you could use, provided they fit in your strategic marketing plan and with your specific target audience.

Direct Mail as a Marketing Tactic

Direct marketing involves targeting a specific message about your service to the consumer. A website is one way to do this, but there are other direct marketing channels to consider like:

- Email marketing
- Direct mail
- Print ads
- Search ads
- Display banner ads

• Radio or television ads

Website

A professional website will help to increase the value of your brand. It gives you an opportunity to give clients a personalized look at your business. Include information about your expertise, background, areas of focus, etc. Keep in mind the learning style of your target audience. Know the level of detail they seek.

Use a blend of elements on your website: images and pictures, video, audio, interactive content, and podcasts are all things you can use to keep your website interesting and fresh. It is important to invest in SEO (search engine optimization). If you have a great site but no one can find it and you don't show up in searches, you'll stay a hidden gem.

Social Media

Social media continues to shape the marketing scene. Some options to consider utilizing include Twitter, LinkedIn, Facebook, Pinterest, and Tumblr. You might also set up a company or personal blog or simply contribute to, or comment on, blogs, and websites related to your industry.

Communicating through social media can be accomplished through writing, by using audio or video, and by becoming known as an expert for your views and opinions. Social media allows you to build a close-knit community of followers. Sites like LinkedIn allow you to gather information about a prospect before you've even met them, or to find the connections your clients or network may have.

Of course, there remain certain compliance issues with social media, so be sure you are consulting with your compliance expert to know what to do and what not to do.

Advertising

Advertising can be very expensive and, in most cases, will not create an instant client base or an immediate, sharp increase in sales. It takes time for advertising to work. For financial advisors, the best form of advertising can be doing it through your niche marketing efforts. For example, if your target is engineers, you could advertise about a specific event or program in an engineering-related magazine. This is often lower in cost, and more direct, than broad-based advertising. To be effective with print or radio ads, you need to repeat them several times, so be prepared to invest in several ad spaces.

Word of Mouth

This is exactly what it seems to be: clients, Centers of Influence, and others are so excited about what you do and the wealth planning services you offer, they simply have to tell others. To jump start "word of mouth," consider speaking at a conference or start a blog to get others talking about your expertise.

Many firms struggle with a long list of things they'd like to do, but only have limited resources to implement their strategy. This is the primary reason why so many plans are never implemented, or are implemented half-heartedly and without the hoped-for results. The marketing tactics plan need not be a lengthy dissertation. It can be a simple implementation plan that shows:

1. What you've selected to implement from the menu of options.
2. What steps you need to take for each item.
3. Who will do what at each step.
4. What costs you will, or expect, to incur.
5. What are the associated timeframes for each item.
6. How you will measure and track success.

Activity: Document Your Marketing Strategies and Tactics

Before you move on, take some time to review your marketing strategy and be sure you are clear on what you are trying to accomplish and what success looks like to you.

- State your desired outcome for your marketing efforts. Do you want to increase client referrals? Expand your niche marketing efforts? Raise your profile?
- Identify the target audience/niche for your firm. Where can you find this niche? What is the best way to communicate with it? What communication materials do you currently have? What materials will you need to create?
- Identify your marketing tactics. What tactics will you commit to? How much will you invest? How will you measure success? What are the next steps in pursuing these tactics?

CHAPTER V
Leveraging a CRM System

> "*The first step in exceeding your customer's expectations is to know those expectations.*"

—Roy H. Williams

S trong client relationships are at the very center of any successful financial advisory firm. But it's not enough to have the relationships. You have to track them, manage them, and share information about them. Customer relationship management (CRM) is a technology that is used to develop those relationships by documenting and then learning about your client's behaviors, wants, and needs.

Diagram 3: CRM System Components

CRM can help to reduce costs and increase profitability by organizing and automating business processes that nurture customer satisfaction and loyalty in the sales, marketing, and customer service fields. CRM systems offer the ability to do the following:

- View and manage account activity and communications;
- Use reports to forecast sales, measure business activity, and identify trends;
- Qualify leads and track prospects;
- Centralize customer data;
- Access, update, and share information across teams and departments.

A CRM system automates and brings rigorous oversight to selling processes. It also:

- Increases salesperson and client support efficiency.
- Raises customer satisfaction, and increases customer retention.
- Optimizes marketing tactics.
- Reduces expenses.
- Anticipates client needs and preferences.
- Improves targeted marketing efforts.
- Provides quicker response time to prospects and clients.

For a CRM system to be effective, you must first identify the important fields for your business. Take notes about what clients are telling you, organize them by type, and have a system of communication outreach. The more personalized this is, the better the data.

Client Segmentation

Client segmentation can make using a CRM much more powerful, because you are organizing clients by themes. In order for client referrals to come easily, and for them to work well on an ongoing basis, you must know your clients and have them segmented by types and categories. Many firms—if they segment at all—will segment based purely upon asset size or revenue flow. That's often called the "Gold, Silver, Bronze" approach to client segmentation, and it has more to do with fee levels than it does with segmenting by needs or characteristics.

Selecting CRM Software

This brings us to the question of which CRM system is most appropriate for financial advisors. The answer isn't simple. It depends on what you need. There are dozens of available programs from which to choose, with new ones arriving every day. You can even have a program custom-made for you. While systems vary, the one you select should have the following, at a minimum:

- **Customer Data Management.** Most systems have a searchable database for customer contact and other information, and storage for important documents relevant to the client.
- **Tracking of Interactions.** The ability to document telephone conversations, meetings, email correspondence, or other interactions is available in most CRM

systems. Some will also track Twitter, Facebook, and other interactions through social media.

- **Workflow Automation.** Standardization of business processes is also commonly available. The process is tracked through a series of calendars, task lists, alerts, etc. Some systems can be set up to automatically schedule the next step in the business process as tasks are completed.
- **Reporting.** Reports are generated by the system to track performance and productivity, as well as forecasting and planning.

Of course, there are programs that perform a whole host of tasks, depending upon your needs and wants. You'll also want to consider these trends when looking for the best CRM system for your business:

- **Social CRM.** This is a way to track interactions through social media. It can be as simple as adding Twitter and Facebook data to a client profile, or it can be complex—a specialized system that taps into social APIs, generating leads and mining for customer attitudes.
- **Mobile CRM.** Mobile apps are becoming more and more popular. These use the unique capabilities of mobile devices, like GPS and voice.

Another consideration when looking at CRM systems is whether you prefer a web-based ("cloud") system or an on-premises system. A cloud-based system is housed on servers managed by a software company. It is usually priced as a subscription and is determined by how many users will need access to the software. An on-premises CRM system is housed on servers in the financial advisor's office. This is purchased as a one-time license with no recurring costs, with the exception of maintenance, upgrades, or customization.

In order to implement a system and make it work for you, it's important to first define your needs, your budget, and your intention for the system. Don't simply take what some other advisor has said works for them. Instead, define your specific needs and then search for the system that fits you. Construct an RFP so you are sure to ask the same questions of all vendors. Make sure they will work with you on implementation and training to identify how your team will use the system and to have an approach that works for all.

Once you have a system in place, enforce usage. Track whether or not your advisors are inputting the information on a regular basis. The data you get out is only as good as what goes in!

CHAPTER VI

Even Non-Sales Professionals Can Sell!

"To me, job titles don't matter. Everyone is in sales. It's the only way we stay in business."

—Harvey Mackay

Who said you couldn't sell? You probably did! The first and most important step to becoming more effective in selling is to remove the idea that "sales is bad" or "sales is sleazy" from your frame of reference. The way we identify or judge something will often dictate how we react to it. If you believe that selling is pushy, or bad, you will resist it. You will shy away from an opportunity to pitch your firm or to go for the close. Selling isn't much unlike dating in that the courting, the wooing, and the asking are all important steps in the process!

Without a clear plan of action and associated names, roles, and expectations, it's a process of throwing a bunch of stuff at the wall to see what sticks. There are thousands of salespeople who take this approach all of the time, and few of them have reliable, successful track records they can point to. More is not necessarily better in sales — rather, targeted, selective focus is the rule.

Many firms also struggle because they create a lot of great marketing materials — brochures, handouts, graphs, charts, websites, and the like — but then they aren't exactly sure where to use it all in the process. Having a clear plan also means identifying your sales process and aligning your materials, as you did in an earlier chapter. What information does your prospect or client need from you at that step? What can you do to reach the next step? Knowing what piece of material you are using, why you are using it, and what you expect to gain from its usage is important before you ever deliver it to an end recipient.

Again, more is not necessarily better. Don't give the prospect more than they ask for or need, and don't overwhelm a client with so much information that if they do have an opportunity for a referral, they don't even know what to say as an introduction. The prospect who asks for "more, more, more" is not necessarily interested—they may just not know what else to do in the process. So be sure to clarify your process up front, and be clear about what you share and expect at each step. A good salesperson is an orchestra conductor; they should be the driver of the effort, and not leave it up to the prospect. For example, whenever you use materials, you don't just hand them over, you show them why this particular information matters to them, and what they can gain from it.

An effective salesperson takes the lead. They manage the process. They don't follow the prospect. In too many situations, each time a prospect says "jump," the advisor asks "how high?" and then becomes frustrated because they are worn out from jumping with no new assets to show for their efforts. You want to identify the process up front for the prospect—remember, you are the expert. You have worked with many more investors than your prospect has worked with advisors.

Too many advisors and professional salespeople shy away from asking, up front, these kinds of questions. Just because the question isn't asked, doesn't mean the answer isn't waiting there to trip you up in the process at some point. The sales process is an engagement. It's a back-and-forth relationship between two people who are both trying to figure out if they should work together. You know from past bad client experiences that not everyone is a good fit for your firm. You are both trying to establish if the relationship will work.

You can be honest with the prospect by saying, "My job is to help you make the best decision." It's not necessarily to help them make the decision to work with you. While most advisors enjoy getting new assets and building their business, having the right client fit is equally important.

To be a sales guru, you want to start thinking of the selling process as an exchange of information. It's not a pitch. It's not a push. It's not a "go for the jugular" approach. Rather, it's like any relationship—an exchange of information about what the prospect needs, what issues they are striving to address, and what decision-making process works best for them.

Because the hardest obstacle in most sales processes for financial advisory services is simply inertia, you will have to learn how to ask for the business. If you believe in what you do and feel confident in your ability to help the prospect and think you offer a high level of service, this should not be hard.

You want to help them, and they likely need your help. Waiting for them to come to that conclusion can often take too long, so you might need to prod them a bit. This is why it's important to get an understanding of their decision-making process and approach. Ask about obstacles so that, when they appear, you can address them.

Be clear on the best way to follow up—"Do you prefer an email or a phone call? What should I do if I am unable to reach you at the time we've agreed upon?" You can also let them know the problems you have seen with other prospects—"It's all too common that an investor needs our services but they become busy or are hesitant to move forward and start the planning process. What can we do together to ensure this doesn't happen with us as you make a final decision?" Remember, you are the expert. Use that expertise to help the prospect make the right decision.

Activity: Ask Prospects the Right Questions

Once you outline your process, you will want to ask the prospect what they need from you to make a decision. Probe on their decision-making criteria and how they typically make important decisions such as this one. Clarify their thinking by asking probing questions:

- How did you make decisions like this in the past?
- What experiences have you had working with a financial advisor?
- What has worked and what hasn't, relative to working with an advisor?
- What information will be most important to you during the process?
- What can I do to make the decision easiest for you, whether you decide to work with us or not?
- What might prevent you from making a decision at this point in time?

CHAPTER VII

Selling Secrets That Work

"*I like to think of sales as the ability to gracefully persuade, not manipulate, a person or persons into a win-win situation.*"

—Bo Bennett

The selling process, to those who have not been trained in it, has its own mystique. The scripts, the proper words at the proper time, and the ability to listen past an objection someone is presenting to you in order to find what they really need are all skills that few people possess naturally. So how does a financial professional—one who wants to grow his business and desires to sell more effectively—do this in a comfortable and effective manner? Let's look at five tenets of successful selling:

The Five Tenets of Successful Selling

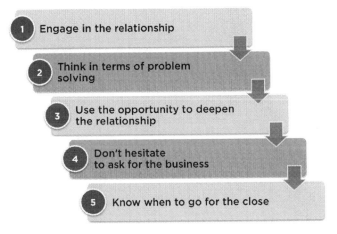

Diagram 4: Tenets of Successful Selling

1. Engage in Relationship

As talked about in the previous section, selling is all about being in relationship with another person, couple, or group. It may be a short relationship if you decide not to work together, or a long relationship if they become a client. It may be a relationship wherein they choose to work with you, or if they do not, perhaps they recommend a family member or friend for your wealth planning services. Many selling terms—for example "the target," "the prospect," or "the close"—sound negative and treat the person trying to make the decision as if they were a fish you were trying to get on your hook. However, if you change the dynamic and the way you think about the selling process, you will change your own attitude to a more positive one. Most advisors are excellent in client relationships—trustworthy, reliable, and honest. Those same skills need to be pulled into the selling process.

2. Think in Terms of Problem Solving

Selling, at its root, is simply solving a problem for a client by offering a solution that meets their needs.

Many businesses have the "if we build it, they will come and buy it" mentality, and they find out too late that not enough people saw the solution to their problems in what was built. Your job is to uncover the underlying problem and understand how your prospect talks about that problem. You want to get a window into why it is a problem, and what success looks like to them.

Most of us don't realize what kind of problems we have until someone brings them to our attention. Think about an inventor such as Steve Jobs. No one knew they needed an iPod, iPhone, or iPad until he sold us on them! So your job in selling is two-fold—you need to ask the right questions to help someone uncover a problem you can solve, and also to paint a picture of what someone might be dealing with that would lead them to need your product, service, or solution.

Life insurance salespeople are particularly adept at this. When a person has their first child, an insurance person can stun them with stories of uninsured parents who left their children helpless and without financial support. Most new parents don't realize this is a problem, but after hearing the horror stories about other young couples, many realize that they have a potential problem for which they need to be prepared. It works the same with financial planning—think of existing clients who came in thinking they didn't have a problem, or identifying the wrong problem, or overlooking some very important information.

3. Know When to Go for the Close

Effectively qualifying and knowing how and when to close is the place where so many professional salespeople falter. In many cases, a suspect or prospect is a warm body who offers an opportunity for a potential sale. As the hope-to-be seller, you may spend a lot of time providing information, following up with phone calls, keeping the person in your pipeline, and assuming there are assets attached that will someday be yours.

The problem is that you don't want to be distracted by people who will never actually work with you. Some prospects may take years to close, so don't immediately walk away from prospects that don't show short-term interest. The longer-term ones may belong on your drip list to send marketing materials and updates to over time. Importantly, though, to determine who is short and who is long term for the close, you need to continually ask yourself, "At this time, does this person have a need or problem they are trying to solve, and do they recognize this problem?" The truth is that not everyone is a prospect: There are people who are simply curious. There are people who are nice and will talk with you all day with no intention to ever buy. There are people who want to shop around and make sure whatever they currently have is the best available. It's your job to focus on the people who are deserving of your time and attention right now, and weed out those who will waste your time with no return on your investment.

As the service provider, you have a right to know at each stage of the process what's happening with your prospect and why. If they ask you for something—brochure, information, to run some numbers, etc.—you can ask why they need it and what they are hoping to gain from it: "Help me to understand your decision-making process. How will you use this brochure? What will you do with it? I'm happy to send it, but I just want to understand your thinking about its importance to make sure it is the best piece for you at this time."

4. Don't Hesitate to Ask for the Business

We often observe advisors not making it clear to a client that they are looking for new business, or to the prospect that they want their business! We all like to be asked—we don't want to be the one to assume the forward position, so be sure you are continually reminding the person how much you'd like their business (or additional business): "My objective is to meet your needs and I am confident I can do that effectively, so I ask that you consider working with me. Are we able to pick a date that we can sign an agreement and start working together?"

Summarize the key points of agreement or benefits acknowledged and ask them if you've missed anything. If not, ask them if there's any reason why they couldn't become a client now.

Many a sale has been lost because the advisor engaging in the process did everything right, but then neglected to actually ask for the business when the time was right!

5. Use the Opportunity to Deepen the Relationship

While advisors talk about the importance of relationships and the depth of relationships they have with strategic alliances and clients, the truth is that there is always room for improvement. Find every opportunity to deepen a relationship by learning more about the person and what they care about, by holding events and providing education they could find useful, and by providing information they can use and share. If an advisor is investing in relationships on an ongoing basis and paying attention to clients and alliances outside of scheduled meetings, the process of asking for referrals and finding new prospects becomes much easier. Make sure you have recorded significant events and milestones for clients. Know their interests and hobbies. Know what information they have and use in financial decision-making, and provide what they need. Find ways to provide value outside of the investment process.

Having new information, material, or updates to share can sometimes be the "ping" that a client needs to pass it along to someone else. Asking a client about a vacation and learning they love to golf is the clue to invite them to your golf club or send them monogrammed golf balls for their next trip. Learning about charitable interests and volunteer opportunities gives you a chance to talk about philanthropy.

Good financial advisors continually work a relationship and find ways to stay top-of-mind to the prospect. While you should qualify and be careful not to waste time, the flip side is that things change in the prospect's life, and you want to remind them you are there and available to help when they need you.

Life is an exchange; in many cases, when you show a sincere interest in them as they are and not as you are, the person will often show a sincere interest in return. If someone believes you can meet their needs, solve their problem, and understand who they are, they will be loyal and committed unless something happens in the relationship.

If followed, these five tenets of successful selling will take your sales abilities to higher levels of success—and as a bonus they will, generally, help to improve your relationships.

CHAPTER VIII

Behavioral Selling

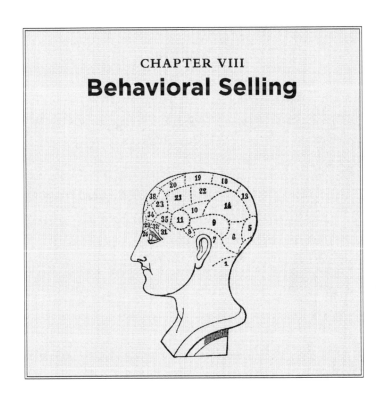

"People's behavior makes sense if you think about it in terms of their goals, needs, and motives."

—Thomas Mann

No matter who is doing it, selling is a relationship business. Have you ever wondered why you can build a good rapport with some clients, but not others? Clients prefer to work with people they subconsciously trust and feel comfortable with. These clients are easy to work with and, in some cases, they'll even help you sell to them. This kind of rapport occurs because you have complementary behavioral styles.

Know Your Behavioral Style

The first thing to do is to recognize that different behaviors exist amongst prospects and clients. You've probably noticed, in your own experience, how one sales approach may have worked perfectly with one prospect, yet you received a very different reaction from another while doing the exact same thing. These differing behavioral styles affect how people want to be sold to, how they want information presented, the amount of information they'd like presented, and how they make their purchasing decisions.

As you've likely already learned, the same approach will not work with everyone. Instead, you must learn to adapt the approach to each client or prospect. This makes them feel more comfortable, and before long, the relationship will improve. You can identify a person's behavioral style by using a process called "DISC." This classifies behavior into four styles which examine our approach to problems, people, pace, and procedures: "Dominant," "Influence," "Steadiness," and "Conscientiousness."

The Behavioral Styles

D: Dominant

People who fall into this category are typically results-oriented. These are the clients who thrive on solving problems. They make quick buying decisions. They tend to be fast paced and they enjoy being in charge. If they are hindered from accomplishing a goal, they become impatient. Those in this category are less people-oriented. These people are easily recognized when speaking. They're more interested in telling rather than asking. They think more in terms of the bottom line. Their facial expressions may also be harder to read than others. When selling to people of this style, make sure to quickly get to the point. They aren't interested in excessive details or in socializing much beyond the niceties. Don't waste their time. Instead, focus on how you can help them to reach their goals. Emphasize results and always let them feel they are in charge. Your presentation should be meaningful and direct.

I: Influence

These are the people persons. They enjoy interacting with others; they are enthusiastic, upbeat, lighthearted, and enjoy humor. These are the eternal optimists —typically seeing the glass as half-full. The can be very persuasive about those things in which they are passionate. You might find them to be outgoing, direct, interactive, and talkative. They speak quickly, are animated, and they freely express their feelings. These people appear to be friendly and casual. They express themselves in a humorous, jovial manner. They add levity to the office with trinkets or fun gadgets. When dealing with this type of person, be sociable and friendly. Match your presentation and pace to their energies. If it's appropriate, take them to lunch and don't be afraid to let them know you like them. With people in this group, you'll need to use personal stories and testimonials about how other people benefitted from your services. Show lots of enthusiasm, and make sure you provide any follow-up work that might be necessary. Make it easy for them to work with you.

S: Steadiness

People who fall into this category also tend to be people-oriented. They just go about it at a slower pace than those in the "I" style. They do not like to feel as if they're being forced to make a quick decision or change. They're excellent listeners, and are patient, calm, and loyal. When a conflict arises, they tend to be the peacekeepers. They focus on cooperating. They are identified by their indirect, reserved approach to others. They may have softer speech and a more open posture. Their facial expressions are often relaxed and warm. They prefer a casual approach. It is important to listen to people in this classification. They need to feel as if you understand their needs. They want to be sure that your firm is oriented toward them, the client. Show that you're interested in a long-term working relationship and that you are dependable. These are the clients who are the most loyal to you when they're contacted by your competitors.

C: Conscientiousness

This group is the most focused on quality. They tend to be slower paced, methodical, and task oriented. Their focus is on the details, and they're mostly concerned about doing things in the right way. These people are analytical, and they frequently set higher standards for themselves. They are more reserved and indirect than the other three groups. They tend to be more formal, with difficult-to-read facial expressions. They do not readily express their feelings. When dealing with this group, make sure your facts are straight. You'll need to be prepared to answer analytical questions, and show references. They really don't want you to socialize with them. All they want is for you to provide them with detailed information so they can make informed, correct decisions. Before they decide, they will thoroughly assess the information you've provided. Focus on logic, facts, and detailed analysis. Formal and slow-paced is the best way to approach this group.

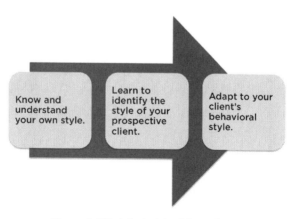

Diagram 5: Effectively Applying Behavioral Styles

Three Key Steps

Most individuals use one or two of these styles, although everyone has the capability of behaving within all four. No style is right or wrong. While each has its own limitations and strengths, there are three steps to use for applying behavioral styles in a selling situation:

1. Know and understand your own style.
2. Learn to identify the style of your prospective client.
3. Adapt to your client's behavioral style.

This works when interacting with someone who has a different style from yours. If they are fast-paced and you tend to be slower and more methodical, you might need to learn to speed up a bit. Conversely, if you are a "bottom line" kind of person who is working with someone who wants to dig into data and get deep in the weeds, you need to accommodate their style. In many cases, the best approach is to team up two people in the advisory firm who are different in communication style from one another but can complement, where necessary.

We worked with a partnership where one advisor was upbeat, direct, and very active in approach, while the other was more thoughtful and methodical. Depending on the type of prospect or client they encountered, they could mix and match styles where necessary. We all can "hear" people better when they communicate in a style we know and recognize. We are often turned off by people who are very different from us. To give your prospect an opportunity to really know you and what you do, you want to match their style of communication and approach.

CHAPTER IX

Increasing Referrals

"In marketing I've seen only one strategy that can't miss—and that is to market to your best customers first, your best prospects second, and the rest of the world last."

—John Romero

Most financial advisors will say they have happy and satisfied clients, but when asked if they receive the referrals they feel they should from that satisfied client base, few are at the number they need and expect. Where is the disconnect? Wouldn't happy clients be thrilled to tell everyone about how you solved their problems? It's important to understand human behavior and how people think. It's simply not enough to "just ask"—you have to create an environment where referrals are a natural extension of the relationship you have with your clients.

Client Referrals

Why are client referrals so talked about in this business but so rarely achieved at a level that the firm feels is adequate? If the numbers are to be believed, industry experts estimate somewhere around 60–70% of new clients come from referrals within the existing client base. This means that 6–7 out of every 10 of your clients is referring someone qualified to your firm.

It would seem intuitive that clients who are happy with their advisor will talk to their friends and tell them to call to make an appointment. The problem is that it doesn't work this way. It's an unusual cocktail conversation indeed when someone rushes up to one of your clients and says, "I have $500,000 to invest—who can you recommend?" Or, conversely, when one of your clients rushes into a cocktail party seeking to talk to their friends about you. As important as the financial aspect of one's life may be, it generally isn't fodder for cocktail conversation. So if they aren't talking about you over dinner, how are the 60–70% of referrals happening every day?

Setting the Expectation

While a client may not rush to let someone else know about your services, they should be made aware that your business relies upon and grows based on how willing your clients are to refer additional business. During the first meeting with any new client, you'll want to ask them to define their view of "success." The conversation goes something like this: "We're only able to be successful on your behalf if we've succeeded based upon your definition of success. I'd like to understand what we can do to ensure this is a successful experience for you." Then begin to record their preferred communication style, need for information, etc.—not just their performance goals!

Once you've gone through this, it's crucial to let them know you grow by referrals. But make sure you do this in a very soft and very non-threatening manner: "Jim, I want to meet and beat your definition of success, and have you so happy to work with us that you'll want to tell all of your friends. We don't ask our clients for referrals; we want to earn your trust and your confidence so thoroughly that you will ask US if we can meet with friends of yours to help them solve their problems. So you need to know that our business grows because we've reached our clients' success goals and they've shared their experience with their friends and colleagues. I look forward to the day you feel compelled to recommend someone to our firm."

That's it. You don't discuss referrals or your need for referrals until this client has reached the stated success goals. You've planted the seed with this client that you grow on the basis that if—and only if—you meet his definition of "success," he will want to find someone to tell about his experience and recommend to your firm.

Secondarily, you need to outline exactly who might be a prospect for your firm. Most advisors assume their clients know. "Someone like you," they might say to a good client. The problem is that I don't know who is exactly like me—who has the same problems I had, the same life situation, and the same stage of financial needs or concerns. Rather than telling the client "I'd like to ask you to refer me to your friends," be clear about who those friends and acquaintances could be. Instead, you might say, "If you have any friends who are about 3-5 years away from retirement and are wondering what else they should be doing to plan for their retirement, please have them talk to me.

"In many cases people think that their corporate retirement account is enough—and it may be, but I could do a review for them and ensure that they are covering their retirement needs with what they have done to date. Do you know anyone who is within that range and nearing retirement?" This way, instead of asking a general question and forcing the client to search their mental database to think about who could be a fit, you focus them on thinking about who they know that might be 3-5 years from retirement and working for a large company. They can more easily go out and identify people with this "problem," and who fits this category of life stage or situation. Clients often want to help and do want their advisor to meet new people, but the clients may not be sure who is right or what they can do to help. Giving them a specific focus or niche to think about can be very helpful.

It's a Process

While you may be setting the table at the outset and letting clients know you are interested in referrals, this is another place where having that brand, that consistent story, and those platform points you use is crucial. Having your message and your market so clearly defined makes it easier to communicate it to your clients, and for them to more easily understand who best fits your firm.

Going back to the cocktail party, while your client may not run around looking for your next prospect, they may very well talk to their wealthy friends and relatives about what you have done, specifically, to help them. This is a very key nuance in selling via referrals. You will want to be so clear with your clients about your process and what you do differently that your client feels they are getting something completely different than they could from every other advisor out there.

Be sure to re-sell. For example, at client meetings, take some time to re-educate your clients on the value of working with you. Find information, education, and events you can hold to deliver useful, actionable material your clients will benefit from. Use those consistent plat-form points to remind clients what you do well, how you solve problems, and for whom you best solve them. The more you repeat it, the more your clients will learn it and be able to repeat it themselves.

It's the human condition to assume the other person knows what we know. Don't assume! Make the connec-tion clear for your client. Walk them through what you did together in planning, in discussing their situation, in understanding their specific needs and concerns, and in meeting those needs and concerns. Don't be like almost every other advisor and confine yourself to performance discussions—talk with them about the experience of working with you. Talk with them about what you've done to help them solve a problem. It's a soft form of re-selling the client on the value of working with you. We all like to feel "smart," so remind your client how smart they are to have selected you to work with.

Define the Market for Them

While your clients probably don't know whether their friends, or even family, meet your requirement of "a minimum of $X in investable assets," they do know the profile of the people they interact with on a day-to-day basis. Make it very clear the kinds of people you are serving in your business. So, as an example, if you specialize in serving women who have gone through a divorce or are widowed, you might share with your female clients, "We have a specialized program we offer to women who have experienced a difficult life change. When someone goes through something unexpected, like a divorce or a death, they are often reeling and don't know what to do to get their financial affairs in order. Our approach focuses on really understanding the person and their situation, and holding their hand every step of the way. We've found over time that our female clients often get a call from a friend or relative asking what they should do, and I wanted you to know we are here for a resource if this ever happens to you." Or if you are holding an event designed for a particular segment of your market—perhaps a business owner seeking to retire but without a succession plan—you can identify your clients who are business owners and let them know specifically how this workshop can help their colleagues who may be worried about their own retirement or succession planning.

Creating Opportunities for Referrals

Review your client base as you did to determine your target market. You are looking for themes and commonalities. Segment them by careers, family situations, business owners, country club members, and so on. There is really no end to the types of segmentation you can do. What's important is that you do it with an eye toward identifying those common themes that will make marketing, communicating, finding referrals, and delivering your message easier and more effective.

As we talked about earlier in this book, once you know who you have in your client base, you can create messaging and opportunities that are clearly designed to meet their needs, and the needs of those with whom they associate. Just be careful to make sure you are positioning whatever you are offering as beneficial for the referring party. Your clients probably want to help someone else they care about to solve a problem more than they want to help you grow your business. In fact, some clients may worry that your attention will be diluted if you grow too much. Instead, frame your requests in terms of helping others: "I know you have benefitted from our planning services; you would not have the insurance trust established had we not worked together, and I know this helps you sleep better at night knowing your children are protected. Do you have other friends or couples with children who might benefit from learning about insurance trusts and how they could protect their family?"

Another approach to take is to explain that you have worked in the industry long enough that you know, in many cases, advisors do not treat investors with the investor's best interest at heart. Let them know you feel you are the best-kept secret, and you are seeking ways to let more people know about what you do and how you do it. Ask them for their help in spreading the word. Ask them for ideas about who to talk to, and how to approach them. Make your client your partner in finding new venues and talking about what you do.

Again, because most people like to help, most will jump at a chance to be of service in some way. If they don't, then know that client may not be a referral source. Go back to the goals you have established for increasing referrals. You probably are not expecting all of your clients to refer; you only need a few to do so on a consistent basis. Find the ones who want to help and focus on them.

Know Their Relationships

If you are creating a plan that includes an emphasis on both client referrals and COI referrals, you may want to start by identifying opportunities to contact the trusted advisors of your existing clients. If you have done your due diligence and recorded all of your clients' other relationships, consider reaching out to the client to let them know—in order to best serve them and ensure communication is flowing—that you will be contacting their attorney, accountant, etc.

When you ask to contact their existing providers, ask the client if there is anything in particular you should share with their trusted advisor about what you do and how you do it. Be sure to convey this connection in a positive framework for your client (after all, it is positive for them if you make the contact!), but seek an understanding from your client about words you might use and the best way to introduce yourself. The benefit of doing this is that you are using the client's words and experience to talk with someone that the client will also be talking with again at some point. By creating a common language, you are making it easier on the two parties (your client and their other trusted advisor) to talk about you and potentially help the advisor to find other clients that might fit your firm. Again, the reinforcement of language and of what you do well helps your message to be conveyed and communicated over and over again.

Activity: Increasing Referrals

To increase referrals, put a systematic approach in place that:

1. Plants the seed up front that your firm grows when the clients are feeling "successful" and eager to refer without being asked.
2. Reminds clients of your message—it re-sells value to make it easy to talk about what you do well.
3. Uses segmentation to find opportunities within your client base and communicate in an ongoing fashion with those segments.
4. Identifies events, or communication, or other outreach activities designed for a particular group in which an existing client will see a benefit for people they know in that group.
5. Finds relationships that already exist between your client and their other trusted advisors that you can leverage.
6. Continues to reinforce your message in a consistent and ongoing fashion.

If you have not identified your goals for referrals, do so now before you begin to implement a plan.

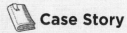

Case Story

One advisor who wanted to increase client referrals and believed he had very happy, satisfied clients in his client base decided to focus on this as a sales strategy. First he reviewed his client base and identified his top ten "should be" referring clients. These were the clients who were (a) happy with him, (b) comfortable talking to others, and (c) connected to the right kind of people he would want to work with in his practice.

He began to contact each of these clients individually and schedule a time for coffee or lunch to discuss the referral process. In one case, his long-term client was shocked that he was looking to grow the business. He had "no idea" the advisor was interested in new clients. He had identified possible connections with each client. One was a business consultant in the local community. The advisor asked about businesses he worked with and whether there were clients with high earning employees who might have a need for financial planning. The client was excited to introduce the advisor to a client of theirs who had recently asked about putting in executive compensation programs. They scheduled a three-way follow-up lunch, and the advisor closed the new client after one meeting.

The consultant/client—who had never previously referred—ending up becoming an excellent referral source and was a Center of Influence sitting inside this advisor's client base. The advisor also continued to reach out to other individual clients one by one and find opportunities for cross-over and referrals.

CHAPTER X

Centers of Influence (COI)

"*I've learned that people will forget what you said, people will forget what you did, but people will never forget how you made them feel.*"

—Maya Angelou

L et's look at developing strategic alliances with Centers of Influence more effectively. Most advisors know that an effective way to obtain referrals is by working with another already established business with a similar target market. These Centers of Influence (COIs) tend to have significant influence with potential clients and can be some of the best sources of referrals.

The idea of finding someone in a complementary trusted advisor role (the divorce lawyer, the high net worth accountant) seems logical on the face of it. The reality of it, as most advisors know, isn't that easy. Remember that just as you are very busy running your business and serving your clients well, the other trusted advisors you endeavor to work with are doing the same. While it can be helpful for them to know of an advisor to refer to when an investment need arises for a client, it really isn't an imperative for them. It's important to keep this in mind when embarking on a COI strategy.

Unless you approach them with a thoughtful "what's in it for them" approach, they may listen very politely and may even like what you have to say, but that alone won't bring you the referrals you are seeking. In fact, too often they will forget all about you once the meeting is over and you won't hear from them again.

Finding the Right Center of Influence

First, it's important to identify what kind of referral would

mplement to your firm. If you are offering
or have an estate attorney on your payroll,
vant to consider other relationships rather
than the tax accountant or the estate attorney.

In fact, don't limit your thinking to attorneys and ac-
countants. Many advisors have successfully created relationships with people completely outside the financial
planning and estate planning realm. Some examples
include high-end real estate agents or relocators, psychi-
atrists or counselors in wealthy communities, real estate
developers, local bankers, insurance agents (particularly
those specializing in long-term care and key man insurance), and others. Consider the relationships you are
willing to invest time in, within your community, and
make a list of the people you'd like to contact there. It's
important to know your area—finding a real estate agent
with time and interest to talk to you in New York City
could be more difficult than finding one in a wealthy area
of Topeka, Kansas.

Once you've identified the contacts you'd like to make,
the next step is to put together a strategy for contacting
them. Make it clear that you are interested in expand-
ing your network—for the benefit of both parties—but
that you want to be sure the relationship and the clients
that might be shared will "match" your firm. You can
introduce yourself via letter or phone call instead of calling "cold," but don't send a lot of marketing materials.
Just a simple, "As a local business owner of an investment
advisory firm, I'm seeking to increase value to my most

important clients. I'd like to meet with you to see if we have mutually compatible goals. I'll call to see if there is a good time to stop by so that we can learn more about each other." Let them know you first want to learn about their business and what they do, who they work with, and what they care about. You are seeking to understand if there is a cultural fit between what they do and what you do.

The first meeting should not just consist of your pitching your firm and telling your story. Rather you should spend the time to ask questions, and identify whether there is a basis for a relationship with them. Don't make the mistake of moving right into your "pitch;" instead, hold back during the first couple of interactions and put the focus on really listening and understanding. You'll find that if you approach the person this way, they'll be the one to start asking you the questions.

Once they've asked about you—and they will if you focus your attention on learning about them—have a short prepared presentation geared to their area of interest to walk through with them. Don't use the same language for the real estate broker as you would with the estate attorney. Using your fundamental 3-4 key platform marketing points about what you do well and differently, take time to craft the message a little bit so that they feel you have designed something very specific to their needs and their clients. Talk from their viewpoint about how your process could serve and benefit their clients. Give examples and tell stories about other clients you have worked with who might have a similar background and set of needs as ones they have described as their clients. The more you've learned about them and what they do upfront, the easier this will be.

Remember that all advisors look very similar to the COI, so they will want to figure out a way to identify something with your style and approach. Make clear the target market you fit best with and the type of client you tend to work well with. Develop a colorful story to explain how you work and with whom you work so that the COI can actually create, in their minds, a "picture" of your process and your approach and the clients that would fit well with you. People love stories, and case studies and examples of what you've done for other clients will be more memorable than a lot of dull data on your research process.

As you go through your presentation, have a section on how you communicate back to the trusted advisor/COI about the work you are doing with their client. Again, use examples of past relationships where you worked very closely with another trusted advisor. Or, if you are implementing a survey process, show the COI the type of information you gain and can communicate back to them to strengthen their own client relationship.

Find out what type of communication the person or firm would like to have from you on an ongoing basis. Are there updates or articles you can send? Is there a newsletter you distribute in which you could include a particular section that would appeal to this COI? Do they need specific materials created (remember the one-pagers you can print on your desktop printer?) that they can give to their clients? Treat the COI as you would a client, and take the time to understand what type of communication works best.

Consider whether you and the COI want to establish written "Rules of Engagement" that define, at a minimum, how you will work together, the values your two firms strive to uphold, and the manner in which you treat your clients. It's important to set expectations between both firms so that you each have confidence about how your clients will be treated by the other.

Everyone is busy—too busy—so, in advance, set up a regular check-in time to review how the relationship between your firms is going. If there haven't been any referrals back and forth, find out why. If there have been, review the process to see what worked well. Review the communication process and determine what else you need to do to ensure it's working well.

Continue to build your relationship. Find educational seminars you can hold together—or that you can hold for their clients at your firm, and they can hold for your clients at their firm. Oftentimes the client of an advisor would love to hear from a long-term care expert, or an expert on housing prices, or even a relationship counselor! As an example, some advisory firms hold sessions with several generations of their clients and have a counselor come in and talk with all of them about meeting goals. In one case, the counselor began to refer her high net worth family members to the advisor in return! In another case, an advisor aligned with a family-business counselor. The counselor, with the client's permission, regularly referred family inheritance and estate issues to the advisor when they came up in family discussions.

Educational events are generally best in person, but you can also offer to do webinars or participate in conference calls to share information the COI's clients may find helpful. Don't make the mistake of "selling" too much if it is designed as an educational event, but also don't make the mistake of educating too much without being sure to include education about what your firm does and how you solve problems for people in their financial lives.

If you have an opportunity to refer to the COI, be sure to call your client to ask about the relationship. Ask them specifically how the COI solved their problem (whatever it may have been). This can help you to understand more about the COI's process and approach. If the client is willing to share, ask them to help you understand what it is like to work with that COI so that you can identify additional prospects.

Conversely, be sure you are asking clients who have been referred to you to give you feedback about their experience working with you. Don't ask if they have had their needs met, or if they are happy. Ask them if you have solved their problem, and if you can communicate back to the COI exactly what they have experienced in working with you. Let them know you'd like to help the referrer understand, in advance, whether someone is a fit or not so you'd appreciate any feedback they could offer. They may not be comfortable talking with you; so if it doesn't go well, ask the COI to employ the same process (checking-in and understanding the client perspective).

Consider sharing a survey between your firms conducted at the point of "intake" when a client joins your firm, or at a regular client meeting. Ask the client what other needs they may have that your firm doesn't meet. If you have established a relationship with the COI and you know each other's firms well—and the product and service offerings—structure the questionnaire to ask about specific items. Does your client want more information about the local housing market? Would they like to understand more about long-term care options? Do they have estate planning needs? Is there a business owner who needs legal support for selling the business? The questions you can ask are endless and can be geared specifically to the COI, and of course you will provide the COI with a list of questions that help them to elicit from their clients the needs that might fit with your firm.

In general, you don't want to have so many COI relationships that you cannot keep up with them. This is another example of where more is not necessarily better. You want to eventually find those 3-5 COIs who are a good fit for your firm and with whom you can establish a good long-term relationship. Treat them like any other important relationship:

- Send them articles or tidbits they may find interesting and useful.
- Call to tell them about a new client and how you solved their problem.
- Call and ask them their advice about something.
- Keep them on your newsletter or email list.
- Take them out to lunch once a quarter to check in and get updates about their business.

 Case Story

In one case, an advisor client had a COI in the office next door, a high-end real estate agent who dealt with executive relocations. The realtor knew the advisor but never referred business. The advisor decided they wanted to deepen the relationship and took the realtor to lunch. The advisor was prepared with all of the issues and concerns most people have when they relocate. He outlined some of the ways he solves these problems and works with people moving into a new area. The realtor was so engaged that she became a client, and started to introduce all of her clients to the advisor just to have an introductory conversation. The advisor continues to find useful information on relocating, moving into a new home and the financial implications, and periodically stops by the realtor's office to deliver some of this information to keep the lines open and active.

✎ Activity: Building COI Relationships

Before you move on, identify those COIs with whom you want to deepen your relationship:

Identify those COIs in your community you don't yet know, but believe to be good partners for your firm:

Develop a list of the steps you will take to learn more about these COIs and communicate with them effectively:

CHAPTER XI
Building a Sales Culture

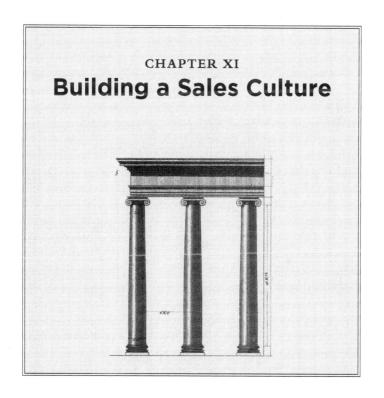

"We must focus on purposes instead of just setting goals, for long-term vision is what keeps us from being frustrated by short-term failure."

—Dan Clark

What does it mean to have a sales culture in your advisory firm? First of all, it means embracing sales—not looking at the selling process as negative or unsavory. It means talking about new business development, meeting regularly to discuss what's working and what's not, and celebrating growth wherever possible.

If your advisory firm lacks a sales culture, in order to be successful in ongoing growth, you must establish one. It's not as easy as saying "we'll focus on sales from now on and everyone needs to be a salesperson!" As a first step, understand that new sales are imperative to the health and longevity of the firm. New sales mean growth. New sales are required if you want to keep the best employees. Great employees leave companies that are not creating growth or opportunities for advancement. Every single employee should be aware that sales equal salaries. They should understand that selling is not just something salespeople do. It's a part of the job of every employee to care that the firm survives and thrives, and to know that they play a critical role in the growth process, whether they are direct client-facing or not. Attitude matters just as much as anything else.

Take the time to actually write down the sales objectives for your firm. This is a critical first step, because most people wrongly assume that just by putting an emphasis on growth—and selling—by definition, they have created a sales culture; but it goes deeper than that. A sales culture has clearly stated objectives, and those objectives are known throughout the firm. They are tracked and measured and communicated.

An effective sales culture means embracing new sales, wanting to grow the business, and being willing to put an emphasis on uncovering new assets. A great sales culture is biased toward action. Don't wait for everything to be perfect before taking action. Create a plan and work with what you have. You can identify 10 "should be" clients, you can find three Centers of Influence to open discussions, you can practice your platform points and telling them more effectively. A successful sales culture is where team members are driven to succeed. Simply put, this means embracing hard work, positive thinking, and persistence as well as a "no excuses" philosophy.

Characteristics of a Great Sales Culture

A sales culture often includes enthusiasm and excitement on the part of team members. People are hungry to learn new ideas, and to find ways to spread the great word about what the advisory firm is doing and can offer. If you don't think your culture is salesy enough, here is a guideline of areas you want to have in place to grow or to develop a more robust sales culture:

- Clearly define and set expectations for growth. Write these down, communicate them clearly to everyone in the firm, and check for understanding among all team members that they are clear about what success

Diagram 6: Creating a Great Sales Culture

looks like.

- Check in with employees to ensure they know how to grow, and that they are clear on the objectives. Ask what they need in order to be a part of the growth culture. Do they need coaching, training, or sales support? Do they need different and more effective materials? What obstacles to growth do they have, and what can you do to help overcome them?
- Ensure communication is active and ongoing. Use the same CRM. Input the necessary information, and make sure everyone on the team is doing so.

Share ideas about what's working well and what's not. Brainstorm ways to move prospects through the pipeline and where to close.

- Be sure everyone on the team knows the core marketing platform points and is clear on how to tell the story. Practice, practice, practice.

- Have ongoing meetings, updates, and conversations about sales. Be clear about what's expected of each employee and how they contribute. Recognize success publicly, and communicate shortfalls to the employee so they know how to correct.

There is really one word that describes how to create an effective sales culture: Consistency. The firm's goals, values, mission, expectations, language, and focus must be in alignment and consistent from one employee to the next—whether they are involved in direct sales or not.

Monitoring Sales Performance

Those firms with the best sales cultures don't stop when they have reached a certain level. They know that one good quarter means you have to work harder to make the next one even better. A regular process of studying and considering sales metrics is important. You can identify trends, both positive and negative, whether it's one person or an entire team, and then implement changes to improve performance. One way to monitor sales performance is through meetings.

Successful Sales Meetings

A sales meeting is an opportunity to motivate and build skills of an entire sales team. In each meeting it's possible to provide an idea, strategy, or tactic to improve sales. Providing some type of reward or positive reinforcement may also lead to better sales results.

Always start the meeting on time. You can start with something fun—maybe reward those who were punctual. This has the added benefit of encouraging attendees to arrive on time in the future.

Keep it simple. Before adding an item to your meeting agenda, ask if it might be able to be completed outside the meeting. Keep the pace of the meeting fairly quick and focused only on the topic of growth and new business development.

Individual updates should follow three concepts:

- Keep the topics compact and succinct.
- Assign timeframes for each piece.
- Capture the future focus and/or lessons learned.

Use the meeting as an opportunity to motivate and reward. Advisors and client-facing staff need to feel appreciated. A simple "thank you" can be meaningful.

Include a capability activity that stretches and challenges the sales skills of the team members. This might focus on generating leads, prospecting, closing, client meetings, networking, etc.

Follow a standard agenda. This will help keep everyone on track and focused. It also has the added benefit of helping to reduce meeting preparation time to as little as 10 minutes. Following these steps can result in consistent, high-value meetings, which will go a long way toward guaranteeing gains in the productivity and results of your sales team.

Weekly Sales Meeting Agenda

1. Successes
   a. Personal development/progress
   b. Firm-wide—what have we accomplished, what are we doing well

2. Closed Accounts
   a. Clients we lost this week—reasons why
   b. What themes are we seeing on lost accounts?

3. Client Meetings for the week
   a. Who are you meeting with?
   b. What is desired outcome of each meeting?
   c. Have you asked for referrals? If not, will you ask?

4. Third Party Meetings for Week
   a. Centers of Influence meetings
   b. Referral Channel meetings
   c. What is your desired outcome for each meeting?
   d. Next steps

5. Pipeline Review
  e. Movement forward
  f. Stagnating deals & brainstorming for movement forward
  g. Movement backward
  h. Identify themes—what's working and what's not?

6. Market Information
  a. Feedback on our services and products
  b. Feedback about company
  c. Competitive updates

7. Obstacles
  a. Personal
  b. Company
  c. Market
  d. Client

8. Management Update
  a. Recent developments
  b. Review of upcoming events

9. Other & Wrap-Up

Diagram 7: Sample Sales Meeting Agenda

Sales Pipeline Management

The system used to sell a product or service is called the "sales pipeline." This sales pipeline has the ability to show the amount of money you will make in the future. It's a terrific indicator of the health of a firm. If you manage the pipeline, you'll stay organized and more in charge of the sales figures. These are some of the things you want to consider in managing a sales pipeline and ensuring that the sales process is working well for your advisory firm:

Number of potential deals added to your pipeline

A pipeline should include all possible prospects and suspects, but the focus should be only on those that are most qualified and could close within a reasonable time frame. Keep the "A" prospects at the top of the list and manage in order of qualification and potential close time.

Average dollar value of a potential deal in the pipeline

This includes the assets under management that can move (i.e., liquid). It's helpful to track this so you can see average deal size of those qualified prospects.

Typical percentage of deals that will make it through your pipeline

These conversion numbers help you determine how you can increase your closing rates. Track at what step most prospects close or where they might fall off the pipeline. Back to the process of identifying your sales steps, you may want to review certain steps if many prospects get stuck in the same place.

Average time it takes for a potential deal to become a paying client

You want this to be as short a period of time as possible! Reducing the sales timeline involves setting clear "next steps" for the potential client. Use action-oriented language. For instance, "After you read the proposal, the next step is..." and explain the next step to the prospect and then confirm time, place, etc. for that next step.

Automate reports in advance using your CRM system

There should be no need to compile sales updates or pipeline forecasts. All the required information should be found in your CRM system. The CRM system should contain dashboards and reports to help focus on those things that need improvement. If the system is set up properly at the beginning, it can save hours of time during future meetings.

Defined criteria and stages

Everyone should be working based on the same designation of a qualified opportunity. They should all know the criteria for considering an investor to be "closeable" in the indicated timeframe. Determining these up front avoids having to ask questions about them in future pipeline reviews.

Separate leads from opportunities

While this is a basic function, it is important. You don't want to spend time discussing opportunities that aren't yet qualified. These don't belong in a pipeline review, as they aren't yet in the pipeline. Only assets under management or financial planning that might be closed in the near term (i.e., within a month's time) should be discussed at this meeting.

Deals at risk

There is no need to discuss potential deals that are on track. It's wiser, therefore, to discuss stalled deals or those that have taken steps backwards. Your CRM report should have already told you which these are, so your time can be spent brainstorming how to move them forward.

Next steps, deadlines, and alerts

The CRM system can be used to assign next-step tasks to responsible team members. If everything is embedded into the same system, it should be easier to track, and the more likely tasks are to be addressed and completed by their owners. Set deadlines for these tasks to be completed, and use the CRM system to send an alert about those tasks that are not completed on time.

Some advisors ask what should be covered at a sales meeting. Below is a sample agenda that can be expanded or minimized depending on your needs. It's good to have a common agenda you will use each time so that everyone knows what's expected, and what to expect. These main categories of information are important to collect. Note how much time you want to spend in each section in advance, and have a time tracker to keep you focused.

Case Story

One advisor who had founded a firm and grown it significantly through his own connections and efforts struggled to create a sales culture. No matter how many times he asked advisors to focus on closing new business, they were not comfortable doing so. He began by instituting a sales meeting once every other week so advisors could come together and discuss opportunities. He had one of the client service reps in the firm oversee the CRM and print out copies of the pipeline so they could discuss prospects. In one meeting, he took the time to have everyone identify if a prospect was an "A" prospect or a "B" prospect and so on.

The advisors began helping one other with ways they were finding new prospects and moving them to closure. One advisor started to work with a sales coach and brought back ideas on how to shorten the sales cycle. They were all excited to share successes at the outset of each meeting, and to help one another brainstorm new ideas for closing.

The founder was pleased to see advisors talking about selling in a more positive fashion. Other team members became involved in the process, and the culture shifted to a growth-oriented, business-building one over time.

CHAPTER XII

Effective Storytelling

"*In the South, we tell stories. We tell stories if you're in a sales position; if you're in a retail position, you lure your customer by telling a story. You just do.*"

—Tate Taylor

Storytelling is as old as the ages. As a child, you probably loved to hear stories. You may have children or grandchildren now that want you to tell the same one over and over again, even though they know how it ends. Stories are compelling. When told well, they draw you in and engage you and make you a part of what's being told. In some stories you may relate to the hero or heroine, and in others you relate to the victim or villain! There are many reasons that stories engage and involve, but from a sales perspective storytelling is important because it can help:

- The prospect to "see" themselves in the story and relate to the client you have worked with in a similar fashion. The more they see themselves, the more real the process becomes for them.
- Bring your story to life—you can give real-world examples of how your platform points are a reality for clients.
- The prospect and client remember stories, and may be able to re-tell stories more easily than just facts and data you may share.
- Your team to talk about what they do in a more personal fashion and connect it to their day-to-day experiences.
- Craft the pitch so it feels more personal and more customized to the prospect and their situation.

Storytelling as Selling Art

Some people are natural born storytellers; they can weave a story out of anything. Give them a time or place, or a subject idea, and they are already drawing you in with specifics and details that make the story come alive. The good news is that you don't need to become a master storyteller for it to work in your sales efforts. In fact, when it comes to financial advisory work, if you embellish too much or paint a picture that is too frightening or compelling, you may put the prospect in a frozen fear mode where they cannot act! You want your stories to show the prospects what's possible for them and to illustrate how you were, and are, able to help meet goals and solve problems.

Storytelling as a sales art helps to move the prospect to action. It helps to illustrate how their problem could be solved, or their life improved. They want to be like the person in your story. They recognize that you have helped someone similar to them, and so you may be the right solution for their needs also.

Storytelling is particularly useful when niche marketing. If you work with a certain group of people and know something about them, you can weave their stories and their experiences throughout all of your marketing materials. You can talk about who they are, what they needed, and how easily you could solve their problem with your experience in similar situations.

To go about developing stories from your ex
base and telling them to prospects, there are a
steps to take:

1. Review the profile of your ideal client or your niche
   market. What's similar about them? Make a list of
   things you can identify — age, geography, career focus, hobbies and interests, philanthropic desires. Paint
   a picture of who they are and what they care about to
   be able to describe them to someone else in detail.
2. Identify the most common needs, desires, or problems of the different niches and markets. Why did
   they come to you? What did you need you to solve?
   What were they looking for when you first spoke?
   This could be different for different groups, so be as
   specific as possible in each niche area.
3. How did you solve their problem and give them a
   solution that worked? What specific steps did you
   take? What insights did you gain?
4. What happened to them after you gave them an
   answer or solved their problem? How did they feel?
   What was their experience post-solution? What did
   they do next?
5. What has been the experience of the client overall?
   Where are they now, and what's working for them
   since you solved their problem?

As an example, let's say you work with the engineers we
talked about in an earlier chapter; you might tell a story
like this:

"We worked with one engineer who had been at the same company for almost thirty years and dutifully paid into the retirement plan, thinking he was preparing for his family's longer-term needs after his last paycheck. Unfortunately he didn't understand enough about the options in the firm's plan, and so he wasn't making the best choices for his situation and his family. When he came to us, he was so depressed and disappointed that after thirty years he was not where he had hoped and needed to be. We walked through his longer-term goals and looked at the decisions he had made.

"While he could have made better choices, he had made a number of good ones. We were able to reallocate many of his funds, and set up an annuity structure to protect his family over the longer term. He was so relieved and thankful that he asked how we could allocate some money in the short term to take his wife and children on an exotic cruise to celebrate while he was still working and able to save.

"We were able to construct a plan to allow him some short-time celebration while also protecting his family for the longer term. His family sent us postcards from all of the ports they stopped in, with a huge 'THANK YOU' written on the front. We framed the postcards, and keep them in our break room to remind all of our advisors of the work we are doing. To us it isn't about portfolio allocation alone—it's about helping people make the right decisions for their family and enjoy the money they make and have saved.

"What plans, hopes, and dreams does your family have that you would love to fulfill for them?"

Stories can be as detailed or as high level as you are comfortable with telling. Just be sure they have a beginning, middle, and end, and that the end is always how you have solved the client's problem and given them a solution that made sense for their needs.

To be most effective, learn something about the prospect first and then tell a story that fits their situation. If they have children and grandchildren, for example, talk about how you have helped a client give to their next generations (if the prospect cares about that); if they have philanthropic interests, talk about how you helped a client leave a legacy for an important charity. Build up a bank of stories that you can tell to the right audience at the right time. The more customized the story, the more the prospect will picture themselves in the starring role!

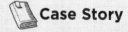 **Case Story**

One advisor was redoing his marketing materials, and during the process of trying to understand his process and his story, we realized that the way in which he talked about what his firm did and how they did it well was to tell stories. He had stories about people who were on the brink of despair and how he had helped them turn their financial lives around. He had stories about couples who were fighting about money and how he solved their financial woes and their relationship ones. He told story after story about his approach, and the happy lives his clients were living.

He had so many stories that it made sense to create a marketing approach based on them. For compliance reasons he couldn't get testimonials or speak of specific clients by name, but he could paint pictures and give backgrounds of the problems, and how he provided solutions.

His website, brochure, and marketing approach began to revolve around the stories of clients and his process in working with them. He was able to make a financial planning process more real and more personal. Clients were able to repeat what he did more easily, resulting in additional client referrals, and he was able to train his younger advisors how to talk about the client stories. He stopped using the traditional "We focus on you" approach, and began to illustrate how it worked in his firm.

CHAPTER XIII

Managing Time to Focus On Business Building

"Time management is an oxymoron. Time is beyond our control, and the clock keeps ticking regardless of how we lead our lives. Priority management is the answer to maximizing the time we have."

—John C. Maxwell

As a financial advisor, you work in a highly competitive field. Each of your days is packed full with any number of tasks, from servicing clients and answering questions to calling prospects and monitoring the markets. All of these tasks are part of the job, and some are more enjoyable than others. When it comes to growth, the more successful an advisor is, the busier they will be!

Oftentimes an advisor will say they are not able to focus on sales because of the other demands they have. While you may plan your day, you may find you are often interrupted or are being pulled in different directions. It's important, to be successful in business building, that you manage your time most effectively. You want to have a plan to integrate selling into your day-to-day, weekly, and monthly plans. In order to do that, you have to have a plan for the day. When you get to work, you want to be ready to start getting things done. Implementing a few time management techniques can help to reduce stress and make for a more productive day.

It starts when you first arrive at the office in the morning. Review what you need to do and select the top three priorities for that day. Review your pipeline, your client requests, and your investment accounts to determine where best to spend your time that day. Instead of being reactive to what comes along, be more proactive by selecting what's most important to you. Once you have identified the top three priorities, create a plan for what you need to do to accomplish each of them. You may, for example, take the time to organize a list of what you need to do to address a client question that awaits an answer, or you may review your COI list and plan to find something that day you can email to one of them to keep the relationship warm.

In order to be most efficient with your time and to focus on those high-gain activities, you will want to know where your time is being spent. The best way to do that is to carry a schedule with you for one week. Record what you are doing every 15 minutes. Do this for a minimum of two weeks. When you can review your activities all at once, and see the time spent on each one, it will give you a good idea of how much of your time is spent on producing results, as well as where time is being wasted. At the end of the week, take a look at what you've written. Put the actual tasks against the stated priorities. How much of what you've done is leading you closer to your goals and matches your priorities? How much seems like wasted time that didn't lead you anywhere? Circle those things that you would do again, and put an "X" through those things that were time wasters.

Ultimately, you can review all of your activities and divide your tasks into categories, such as:

1. **High Priority and High Urgency.** This would include things with strict approaching deadlines.
2. **Priority but not Urgent.** Things like training classes, networking, etc.
3. **Less Priority but Date Certain.** Anything that

needs a response by a certain date—club meetings, sporadic email messages, and so on.

4. **Not a Priority.** This would include fantasy football, water cooler conversations, etc.

Anything that really matters is in the first bucket, and should have a time assigned to it. Create blocks of time for high-priority conversations or tasks, scheduling a beginning and end time. Plan to spend a minimum of 50% of your time in those things that produce the most results. Make sure to leave time during the day for interruptions, but do not respond to people on auto-pilot. Think about whether you need to respond right away and whether it is the best use of your time. While you may not want to say "no" to clients, or even employees, you can state a reasonable time within which you will get back to them and answer any questions. Be in control of your time; don't let others control it for you.

During the last 10 minutes of the work day, make a list of the action items for the next day. Number them according to importance and prioritize them. Be ready to focus on your top three priorities at the start of the next day.

Multitasking

In finance, success often depends on the ability to deliver critical research or reports that require accuracy and timeliness. Success in finance boils down to one's ability to always deliver on critical and immediate deliverables.

Many advisors tend to spend too much time on unimportant tasks. When all is said and done, no one really cares about how many email messages you sent and received, the social activities in which you participate, or the order of your filing system. What is more important is what you might deliver to help your clients or your organization. Submitting an audit report on time, accurately calculating net present value for a project, or making sure Excel formulas provide accurate totals are more important.

Success involves simplicity in how you approach your work. It is better to first, complete the important, urgent, difficult, and highest-value items. Do only one thing at a time and do not stop until it is finished. This is a much more efficient way of finishing tasks, as it does away with having to constantly start over again to take care of smaller, unimportant tasks. If it's a large or long-term project, then separate it into smaller portions. Remember this adage: "How do you eat an elephant? One bite at a time!"

Email Inbox

Your email inbox can be a significant time waster. To stop wasting time checking unimportant email messages, set aside specific times to check your email, preferably no more than three or four times throughout the day. Place any email that is not urgent, but needs a response, in an after-hours folder. Make it a point to respond to only the most critical, work-related emails during your workday. Make sure your inbox is empty before you leave work.

If there are messages that need attention by the next day, then place those in a folder labeled "Urgent." Add those to your "to do" list for the next day.

Utilize the "rules" function if you have it. Have emails go into a folder right away and organize them by type of sender. You can create folders for just "Clients" or for each individual client. Create a folder called "Needs Response" and put emails in there that require your attention but that you cannot respond to right away. If you send an email to someone and are waiting for a response, create a folder called "Waiting for Response" so that you can easily check what's outstanding. Make the best use of your email system so that you control it and it does not control you.

Delegate

Whenever possible, assign tasks. If it's something that you absolutely do not have to handle yourself, assign it to someone else on your team. You should do only those things that require your attention or expertise. Some people are better at delegating than others. As a rule of thumb, you should identify those tasks that you do not like to do or are not good at. These are the things that will often slow you down and keep you away from doing what you need to do.

Be creative—if you cannot hire resources, consider a virtual assistant, or outsource through a website such as guru.com, fiverr.com, or elance.com. There are people who can do most anything—you may just need to search a bit to find them!

 Case Story

One advisor kept wanting to focus on business building, but every week at the end of the week she ran out of hours and could never seem to make it a priority. We asked her to do the time-tracking exercise. She was frustrated and did not want to do it because she felt it was "just another distraction." However, she agreed to do it for two weeks and then review the results.

At the end of that time she was astonished at how much she was doing that fell into the "not priority" category. She was a people-pleaser and found she was allowing team members to call her and walk into her office all throughout the day. She would stop what she was doing and focus on their problem, and give too much time at any point. She had no boundaries established, and people were used to her being there for them. Once she realized how much time was going nowhere, she set down parameters. She held "office hours" when she was available, and asked that all non-urgent matters be addressed during this timeframe. Once team members realized they could not access her any time they needed, they started to solve many of their own problems and became more productive. She was able to take the time she had gained and use it to focus on her business-building efforts.

CHAPTER XIV

Ongoing Communication
to Deepen Relationships

"Get closer than ever to your customers. So close that you tell them what they need well before they realize it themselves."

—Steve Jobs

You've learned by now that selling is really extending relationships. It's no secret that relationships stay solid because trust and loyalty are developed. If a client trusts you and feels confident about the choices you are making on their behalf, they will stay with you for the long haul and probably participate in your efforts to grow.

One of the most effective ways an advisor builds long-lasting trust with their clients is through effective and consistent communication. Client communication, when done well, is a very effective sales tool. When used for business-building purposes, you want to think about varying communication in style, timing, and approach. The more the clients hear from you and you reinforce the good decision they made to work with you, the more they may remember to refer and support your business-building efforts.

Methods of Communication

Varying communication means using a number of different mediums and delivering information at different times. It means looking beyond the packaged newsletter, along with the annual meetings and the quarterly statements, and calling this varied communication. These effort must be complemented by a number of other outreaches to let clients know you care about what they think and you want to communicate proactively with them. Here are some other ideas to keep in touch and keep the

...unication open:

...ed email communication delivering a message ...t your perspective on the market and what changes you might be making to your approach, or your strategy based upon market conditions. This could include observations about the market, and how your philosophy and approach is working in concert with market movements.

- A calling cycle for clients just to discuss what's happening in their lives and to see if they have any questions. If set up on a periodic and regular basis, it makes it easier to call no matter what's happening in the markets. It's best if you can find a reason to call—this could be anything from some change in their lives, to recognizing their birthday. It's an excuse to make the connection.

- Communication in the form of articles, links to newsletters, books, or other interesting information sent to those clients for whom the material would be useful: the client with the mother entering a nursing home, the young couple about to have their first baby, etc. Be creative with this one! Don't overload any one person with information, but selectively find an opportunity, at least once during the year, to provide something targeted and very specific to a client.

- A client survey—either online or by phone—to gather input and understand what's working well for your clients and where you might want to make changes.

- A letter or email, or both, sharing some of the

feedback from the survey and letting clients know exactly what many of them are finding valuable. You can also use this feedback to determine what you are going to change in response to their input.

- A communication from one of your COIs or other trusted partners; something they've written that might be valuable to a number of your clients in another area of their lives. If you can create a piece together, it's even more powerful, and can also be sent to the COI's client list.

- An audio CD or online program with your voice talking about what's happening in the markets and what your firm does differently than others in working with clients.

- A client call-in opportunity where clients can call and listen to the portfolio managers and ask questions about the process or the markets.

- A handwritten note simply to say, "Thank you for being a valued client."

- An email communication or letter sent with an updated marketing piece reminding clients of what you do well and how you can help their friends and families.

- A LinkedIn announcement about something you think they would enjoy learning about or participating in.

Building Trust

When you are doing the initial intake session, and then periodically as you meet with clients, ask them what medium of communication is working well for them, and what else they'd like or from which they might benefit. Conversely, also ask if there is something you are providing they don't find beneficial and would like removed.

Again, it is critical to have a tracking system and to be able to tag clients and create lists of the email types by segment, calling cycle, etc. You can create a "menu" of communication options and ask them which ones they are most interested in. By tracking their interests, it's another way to show that you care about communicating with them in a way that works for their needs and interests.

Surveys to Learn What They're Thinking

We've already established that, for a financial advisor to be successful, they must have the ability to draw in, understand, and address the distinct needs of their clients. Another part of that success is being aware of what their clients are thinking. Never assume your loyal clients are satisfied clients. Are they happy with the services provided? What can the firm do better? What new products and services would the client like to see added? One of the best ways to learn the answers to these and other questions is through a client satisfaction survey.

There are a number of methods by which to conduct a client satisfaction survey. You can use an online survey company or an online market research company to conduct the survey for you. In-person focus groups, mail, email, and telephone interviews are other options. Whatever method you choose, it's important to plan. Know what you want to learn from the survey; be very specific about the kind of feedback you hope to receive. Make sure to identify your target group—do you want to survey new clients, long-term clients, etc.? Asking the right questions on the survey is paramount. Be specific, but keep the questions simple.

It's important to act on the information received. Correct the things that need correcting, and research new products or services they may have mentioned. Be sure to thank your client and let them know their answers were received and being acted upon.

For best results, it's wise to conduct client satisfaction surveys once every other year. This allows you time to implement any feedback you may have received, to on-board new clients, and to see what kind of changes are happening over a 24-month period.

Client Advisory Board

Implementing a client advisory board can help a financial advisor to better understand their clients, as well as get valuable feedback about how to improve. Another benefit is that client advisory board meetings can be a source of referrals for the advisor if used correctly. There are many goals for a client advisory board, but for selling purposes or business building, you gather together a group of clients from different segments to provide insights and ideas on how best to grow the firm, what's working and what's not, and what changes you might want to consider making.

The first step is to establish the board. You'll need to schedule the meeting, choose a facilitator, and find a venue. Next, choose a mix of 7–15 of your best clients. These should be the type of client you'd like to continue to work with. Call them personally to invite them. Make sure they know they'll be meeting with other clients. You might also let them know they don't have to talk about any topic, nor disclose any information with which they are not comfortable.

At the start of the meeting, introduce the topic and your key objectives, and set the ground rules. Take them through the agenda you have prepared prior to the start of the meeting. Discussions can go off track, but bring them back in line if it strays too far from the topic at hand. Have the facilitator ask the tough questions. Take notes during the discussion—even if you disagree or don't like it.

After the meeting, immediately talk with staff members who attended to get their feelings and feedback while it's still fresh in their minds. If necessary, schedule a staff meeting to review feedback and create a plan of action.

Send a summary letter to the clients who participated. Include key points, and who will be following up on them. Reassure them that every suggestion will be evaluated, and some will be implemented. Be sure to thank them for participating.

 Case Story

One advisor who was stymied in his growth efforts decided to establish a client advisory board and seek counsel from his clients: Why were they so happy and satisfied, according to the surveys he'd done, but they didn't refer? He found when he brought them all together that:

- They had no idea he wanted to grow, and were uncomfortable asking him to talk to new connections they had.
- He was not giving them adequate opportunity to pass along information—there was nothing they could reuse or resend to their contacts.
- They wanted to help with growth efforts and became very engaged in the process.

CHAPTER XV

Generational Selling: Crossing the Divide

"Each generation imagines itself to be more intelligent than the one that went before it, and wiser than the one that comes after it."

—George Orwell

In today's advisory firm there might be up to four generations working side by side, with a fifth one waiting for their turn. Many practices want to extend the relationships with their clients' kin and focus on multi-generational selling. However, the same approaches don't work for each of the generations, so if you want to sell to more than one, and keep those relationships intact, you need to understand them.

Every generation has a shared history and core belief system. Each has different needs and preferences. All generations have their own traits—hairstyles, music, clothing preferences, and even vocabulary. They also have particular likes and dislikes, as consumers, in how they prefer to be approached, pitched, and sold the products and services they are offered. Sometimes the differences between the various generations are minor; others can mean losing a sale. Your methods of communication, too, may seem perfectly normal to you, but they may be seen as pushy or intrusive to others. Worse, to someone in a younger generation, you may come off sounding like a parent!

These generational differences are more pronounced today, simply because people are living longer. There are more generations alive today than at any other time in history. Add to that the fact that our world has made significant changes over the past 75 years or so. Those who grew up in the 1930s had a very different life experience than those who grew up in the 2000s and the generations in between. These groups can be broken down as follows:

Silent Generation (1925–1945)

They witnessed World War II in childhood, and the Civil Rights Movement. They bought just about everything— insurance, clothing, furniture, and food—from business owners who were also their friends and neighbors. Stores and shops were, generally, locally owned and not part of a national chain. The salespeople with whom they did business were fair, courteous, ethical, and skilled in exceptional customer service.

Baby Boomers (1946–1964)

They saw space exploration first hand, as well as the first modern "counterculture." They are the largest consumer group in the U.S. Of all previous generations, they are the wealthiest, healthiest, and best educated. They don't like having their time wasted.

Generation X (1965–1985)

This group witnessed the Vietnam War, the cold war and its end, and the rise of mass media. This is the world's first computer generation. They're more likely to research online prior to making a decision about a purchase. These are also the generation without a lot of time to spare—they're busy juggling careers, marriage, and family. They are more likely to have a greater emphasis on family and household responsibilities. They prefer quantity over quality when it comes to their children. This generation tends to be very concerned about the environment. They aren't as financially secure and don't enjoy the same job stability as previous generations did. They're better educated than previous generations, yet are more pessimistic when it comes to discussing their financial futures. They do not expect to receive retirement pensions.

Millennials (1978–1994)

This group saw the rise of the information age, the internet, and the war on terror and the Iraq War. They've also witnessed rising prices. They've grown up surrounded by technology, so they might be considered the "tech generation." As youngsters, their parents allowed them much more purchasing power than previous generations. As a result, they are also much more marketing savvy.

Generation Z (1995–2007)

This is the newest group of consumers. They've seen the rise of the information age and the expansion of the internet, witnessed the dot com bubble and digital globalization. They are young, and more likely to live at home and still receive financial support from their parents. If possible, they prefer to live in cities and trust their friends' opinions, above all else, when determining which things to purchase.

It's obvious that each generation has had different life experiences. Understanding how these experiences affect each group is necessary, in order to smoothly transition in dealing with a member from one generation to that of another. Remember, too, that within each group are differences in beliefs, behaviors, and attitudes. While there is no one best way to sell to any particular generation, there are methods that work best for each.

The Silent Generation

A sense of connectedness is very important to this group, and that doesn't just mean family. Human interaction is important to these Silent consumers. Look them in the eye when addressing people of this generation. They appreciate honesty and transparency. People in this group are readers; a Pew research study noted that 81% of people aged 65 to 74 and 86% of those over 75 read something (book, magazine, newspaper) within the 24 hours previous to participating in the survey.[1] That does not mean, however, that they're interested in reading long-winded advertising copy. Their time is valuable to them. Images are important to this group.

They also do not appreciate being rushed or pressured into purchasing. When speaking to them, it's important to speak slowly. Sure, they can keep up with you, but younger people tend to talk faster, which can make the Silents feel rushed. They value personal testimonials. If you want a good recommendation six months into the future, make sure you portray yourself as someone who is putting them first and yourself second.

---

1   "Marketing to the Silent Generation," *The Agitator* (website). Retrieved from http//www.theagitator.net. Accessed on May 17, 2014.

Baby Boomer Generation

Baby Boomers tend to think they are in a market segment of one. These are the more demanding and curious clients. They are more apt to be self-reliant, and have a great appreciation for that trait. They make purchases to please themselves and don't worry about what other people think. Baby Boomers are looking for common courtesy and integrity from those from whom they purchase. In general, they've endured every sales method out there, and they don't fall for scripted pitches or fluff. They've heard it all before. They won't easily fall for tricks, so it's best to not even bother trying. They want to trust you, so empathy and honesty will go a long way with this group. They tend to be tremendously loyal to companies with whom they have a good relationship.

Baby Boomers tend to respond well to emotions and memories. Mass advertisements do not appeal to this generation. Boomers prefer marketing that is targeted toward the entire shopping experience, rather than just the product or service being offered. In general, they want more information about products and services, but don't oversell what you can do for them. They prefer this information to be presented in a no-nonsense manner as opposed to glitz and glamour. They avoid frills, and are more interested in comfort over style.

Those in this generation want to be heard; therefore, it is vital to listen to their wants and needs. When dealing with someone from this group, give them your undivided attention and avoid multitasking. They are aware that retirement is "just around the corner," but they are resistant to anything associated with old age or infirmity. That's where empathy and honesty can be helpful. However, never call a Boomer "old." That's an automatic sales killer.

Generation X

This is a more complex generation of people who have very specific wants, needs, and values. They aren't rude, but X-ers don't place the same value on courtesy as do previous generations. They're more interested in getting from point A to point B as efficiently as possible. "Efficiency" is their goal. They are looking for value and permanence. In all income levels, they are more cautious in their spending habits and love to talk about how much they have saved. They are tech savvy, and will tell their friends, family, and co-workers when they find a great deal. If you're offering something that an X-er deems valuable, you can expect to hear from their contacts as they spread the word. They place great value on the opinions of their friends. They know the sales tactics that have been used in the past. New, different, and exciting will grab their attention.

More than any other, this group is drawn to affordability and quality. This group is not easily manipulated. They are unimpressed by direct advertising, mass media, and hype of any kind. They consider hard selling to be poor selling. Instead, it's better to get them to listen. Before making a decision, they want to know who you are and what you stand for. They want to know about your business and, as previously mentioned, they're interested in quality. While they tend to be somewhat inflexible, it's important for the salesperson to remain flexible. If they're undecided about your services, listen for ways you might cater to their needs. Communicate to Generation X-ers on a personal level. For example, an email message with their name in the header makes a Generation X-er feel as if they are important to you.

Millennials

Millennials are becoming the most important demographic in the U.S. Unfortunately, they don't really want to hear about your business. They are probably the most challenging of all the generations. Those in this generation do everything online, and that includes buying. To this generation, good customer service means you have an app they can use. Text-ing with a salesperson is their idea of having a close business relationship. They tend to trust what they see online, and are huge users of social networking sites like Facebook. However, it's important to know which sites to use for selling purposes. They get annoyed if they feel their online spaces have been invaded. This generation and Baby Boomers may seem alike in some ways, but there are some very important differences. For one, this generation doesn't take things quite as seriously.

Millennials want you to sell to them, but they are not loyal to brands. They'll drop a brand as if it never existed if something better comes along. To a Boomer, that's disloyal. To a Millennial, it's common sense. If you do earn their loyalty, be prepared to continue to earn it. This group wants consistent value, and they will leave if they feel they aren't getting it. They are not interested in warm, fuzzy stories; they have no interest in small talk. They tend to respond favorably to marketing that gets right down to business. Authenticity matters to Millennials. Don't try to play them. They appreciate when you authentically present your brand. This generation is skeptical. They fact-check everything and they'll use multiple sources. Get your message told quickly. Keep online video campaigns under two minutes in length. Being quick, brief, and descriptive works with this generation. Want Millennials to share your message via social media? Make it emotional and authentic. Television advertising is a waste of money with this group. They hate commercials and won't watch them unless there is a reason. Even then, they'd most likely watch it online, through Hulu or YouTube.

Generation Z

This is the up and coming "digital" generation. In just a few years, this group will have the most buying power. They are extremely bright, flexible in nature, and diverse. Generation Z-ers don't want to be told what to buy or how to do it. It annoys them. They tend to be less trusting than other generations, and will turn to their friends when trouble strikes. This group tends to have more leisure hours in a week, which they use to participate in their favorite pastimes. Generation Z is tech savvy and is connected to everything: friends, entertainment, and data. Social media, instant contact, social causes, and social justice are very important to them. They prefer interactive media and want multi-functional gadgets. Generation Z-ers prefer websites, social media, and apps that allow them to post videos and pictures, text, comments, ratings, etc. They are not loyal to any one brand. Marketing to this group might involve some of the following:

- Make use of technology-based marketing and sales channels like text messages, apps, mobile internet, etc.
- Make product information available online, keeping it easy to get to (no more than two clicks) and the information clear, concise, and short.
- Promote social responsibility.
- Use Facebook, YouTube, Twitter, etc.

As with everything we've talked about in this book, be deliberate in your efforts. Identify those clients where you have not yet connected with their next of kin. What do you know about their family? What ages are the people you need to reach? Have a plan. In many cases, it helps to have different ages of advisors working on the same family account. Like attracts like, and your 35-year-old advisor may do a better job of reaching out to the "children" of your patriarch client than you might be able to do. Stay attuned to their needs and respect them.

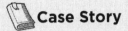 **Case Story**

One advisor who wanted to work with the next generation of a client's family refused to put client reports and updates out on the web. He didn't believe in mobile apps or investing in technology. Once the younger family members, ages 26 through 32, learned they could not access information in a quick and easy fashion by using technology, they took the money they had inherited and moved to another, more advanced advisor. The moral of this tale: Know your audience and stay one step ahead of their needs.

This advisor ended up hiring a younger advisor who focused on implementing technology and approaches that would appeal to the younger generation. He assigned his junior advisor to reach out to the next generation of most of his families. He was able to "save" a number of other situations by establishing a firm relationship with someone who understood the needs, spoke the language, and connected well with his clients' children and grandchildren.

CHAPTER XVI

Creating a Sales Program for the Next Generation

"*Each new generation is reared by its predecessor; the latter must therefore improve in order to improve its successor. The movement is circular.*"

—Emile Durkheim

With many in the older generations retiring, the Millennials are beginning to make up a large portion of the workforce. Some Millennials are even entering higher-ranking positions where they have a great deal of responsibility. One of the biggest challenges for advisors is determining how to bring onboard and train this generation of workers. It's becoming an imperative, because there are many more advisors getting ready to take their own retirement, and not as many new advisors coming in to fill the void. Learning how to train and coach the next generation of staff is going to be important if most advisory firms are to survive the departure of the founder or lead advisor.

Many an advisor has believed they have found their successor, only to have that person leave long before the transition was to take place. It's not enough to manage someone from the next generation the same way you were managed. The adage "that's how I learned and how I did it," might actually do you in! Millennials are different from the Baby Boomers they are following in the practice. In most cases, they want instant gratification and frequent feedback. They expect their careers to progress quickly. They've always received constant praise from their parents. They believe there are no losers, and that everyone is equal. Everyone wins a trophy. While they are eager to learn, they want meaning in what they do, so cultural values are very important to them and doing the right thing can be, as well.

While they might believe everyone wins, this group is

very open to feedback and coaching to help them improve. This mindset offers an opportunity of providing them information about best practices, as well as an opportunity to critique their performance—as long as it is presented as an opportunity for development. This generation of workers prefers having clearly defined expectations. Thoroughly outline your expectations and their duties on a daily basis. They prefer to know how their performance will be evaluated and the criteria being used for that purpose. Minimize miscommunication by conveying clearly what is expected of them throughout the training process.

Millennials benefit from a comprehensive training program. This group of workers responds very well to training based on the visual. They prefer information that is easily absorbed through presentations or infographics. Online training courses might be used to teach the basics and company policies. This may even help to make the learning curve shorter. They are much more comfortable learning virtually, through online discussions, websites, and videos. They have no trouble in researching through online sources. They prefer fast-paced, interactive programs.

As with anything, making progress toward greatness takes time. This is particularly true with Millennials. Training is a process that takes time.

Millennials are usually very eager to learn and generally come to a training program with a positive mindset if they understand beforehand how attending the session will improve their performance.

When a Millennial first starts to work with your organization, you may want to give them authority over just a small area and then gradually increase their authority as they prove themselves. You may want to monitor them via an eLearning program. This is an effective way to gauge their progress, and to point out areas where improvement may be necessary.

Reverse mentoring is something to consider when training Millennials. Because of their youth, their strengths may be overlooked; yet, they have technology skills that older generations lack. They're great at networking using social media and online collaboration. They are also very good at multitasking. Their knowledge of technology is a serious asset simply because most businesses today utilize cloud computing, high tech software, analytics, and so on in their daily operations. Millennials are likely to very quickly grasp new technology. That said, Millennials may be able to teach the older employees about technology.

When training Millennials, it's best to be flexible. Being too rigid with them can be a hindrance to their progress. In one case, an advisor thought he had found the perfect successor. The advisor was 57 years old and hoping to retire at 62. The young advisor, 33 years old, seemed "just like" him when he was starting out. The younger advisor wanted to know how to succeed. How many years would it take? What milestones did he need to reach? How would he be measured and rewarded? The older advisor wanted him to "trust the process" and do what was asked without a firm commitment. He wanted the flexibility to cancel the transition if he didn't like the way things were going. Unfortunately, their differing needs caused a great divide between the two advisors. They ended up distrusting one another and could no longer work together. The younger advisor started his own firm, and the older advisor still seeks the perfect successor to work alongside him.

If you want to create a plan for sustainability for your advisory firm, you have to focus on the needs of the next generation (or two or three generations) and work with them in a way that's meaningful to them. Most people, irrespective of generation, want to succeed and want to do their best, but they measure what that looks like and how it should work very differently depending on the era in which they were raised.

Give your younger staff members the tools and training they need to succeed, and communicate clear expectations and measurements. In the long run, it will be important for all parties involved.

CHAPTER XVII

Next Steps:
Your Sales Success

"*Always be closing… That doesn't mean you're always closing the deal, but it does mean that you need to be always closing on the next step in the process.*"

—Shane Gibson

There has been a lot to digest in the pages heretofore on creating a sales culture, assessing your practice, and turning yourself or your advisors into successful salespeople. As stated, with regard to having a sales plan and a strategy for success, you want to take the time to outline your specific next steps and how you will use the information you have learned herein. First, consider what you've learned. Maybe you need to:

- Further hone and define your brand and platform points
- Create a sales strategy
- Communicate a sales strategy and your goals to your team members
- Develop a plan to support the strategy
- Identify your targeted clients for referrals, or Centers of Influence
- Create a sales culture
- Hold ongoing meetings and open communication about growth activities
- Work on your time management to allow ample time for selling
- Outline your effective sales process
- Identify those marketing materials that coordinate with your sales process
- Create the materials you need for effective selling
- Update your website, your pitch book, or other marketing pieces
- Find new and innovative ways to communicate with your clients and Centers of Influence
- Hone your qualifying skills with prospects

- Teach your next-generation staff members how to sell more effectively
- Work with multi-generational issues within your client base

Other Things You Want to Focus on and Consider

Check only 1–3 things that you will choose to focus on first. Next, create a clear step-by-step plan for addressing these things. Don't just put a line on a piece of paper saying you are committed; instead, put together a plan as you would a portfolio. Consider the components:

- What has to happen first, next, and so on?
- Who should be involved?
- What costs might be incurred?
- What deadlines will you assign?
- How will you check in on progress?

To be committed to growth, and to become the successful salesperson that your practice needs you to be, you must have a plan of action that you can identify, commit to, and follow through on. Keep this plan in a prominent place, and continue to work on refining your skills. It's unfortunate, but true, that a new business development effort requires trying some things that will ultimately fail. A well-orchestrated business building effort, over time, contains many components. But there isn't one size that fits all, and not all individual efforts work well within all firms. Some firms find they are focusing on one area more than others over time. Some firms continue to do many things and enhance all of them. If you find you can't commit the time and resources to ensure success, you may need to abandon one effort in favor of another.

Too many firms will try something hoping for a "quick hit" but, particularly in the wealth management business, those aren't easy to come by. It's a relationship- and confidence-building business, and it does take time to see the results of the seeds you are sowing.

Selling is one of the oldest professions around, and for good reason. People have problems and they need someone to solve them. They value the person who can listen, understand, and then offer a solution to quell their pain or increase their pleasure. You offer a service that most people need. Refine your selling process and skills to allow yourself to let more people know what you do and what you can do for them.

And, sell on!

Additional Reading

Diagnosis: The Sales Effectiveness Model

Benson, James M., and Paul Karasik. *22 Keys to Sales Success: How to Make It Big in Financial Services*. Princeton: Bloomberg, 2004.

Gitomer, Jeffrey, Luhong Sun, and Jeffrey H. Gitomer. *The Little Red Book of Selling: 12.5 Principles of Sales Greatness*. Austin, TX: Bard Press, 2004.

Griego, Michael. *42 Rules to Increase Sales Effectiveness*. Cupertino, CA: Super Star, 2009.

Standing Out in a Crowded Market: Brand Effectiveness

Aaker, David A. *Building Strong Brands*. New York: Free Press, 1996.

Bradlow, Eric T., Keith E. Niedermeier, and Patti Williams. *Marketing for Financial Advisors: Build Your Business by Establishing Your Brand, Knowing Your Clients and Creating a Marketing Plan*. New York: McGraw Hill, 2009.

Ries, Al, and Laura Ries. *The 22 Immutable Laws of Branding: How to Build a Product or Service into a World-class Brand*. New York: HarperBusiness, 1998.

Stiff, Dan. *Sell the Brand First: How to Sell Your Brand and Create Lasting Customer Loyalty*. New York: McGraw-Hill, 2006.

The Power of Niche Marketing: Finding Your Natural Niche

Friedmann, Susan A. *Riches in Niches: How to Make It BIG in a Small Market*. Franklin Lakes, NJ: Career, 2007.

Reynolds, Don. *Crackerjack Positioning: Niche Marketing Strategy for the Entrepreneur.* Tulsa: Atwood Publications, 1993.

Marketing Strategy and Tactics

Bradlow, Eric T., Keith E. Niedermeier, and Patti Williams. *Marketing for Financial Advisors: Build Your Business by Establishing Your Brand, Knowing Your Clients and Creating a Marketing Plan.* New York: McGraw Hill, 2009.

Ries, Al, and Jack Trout. *The 22 Immutable Laws of Marketing: Violate Them at Your Own Risk.* New York: HarperBusiness, 1993.

Weinberg, Gabriel, and Justin Mares. *Traction: A Startup Guide to Getting Customers.* S-curves, 2014.

Leveraging a CRM System

Drucker, David J., and Joel P. Bruckenstein. *Technology Tools for Today's High-margin Practice: How Client-centered Financial Advisors Can Cut Paperwork, Overhead, and Wasted Hours.* Hoboken, NJ: John Wiley & Sons, 2013.

Iyer, Gopalkrishnan R., and David Bejou. *Customer Relationship Management in Electronic Markets.* Binghamton, NY: Best Business, 2004.

Even Non-Sales Professionals Can Sell!

Baer, Jay. Youtility: *Why Smart Marketing Is about Help Not Hype.* Portfolio, 2013.

Griego, Michael. *42 Rules to Increase Sales Effectiveness.* Cupertino, CA: Super Star, 2009.

Pink, Daniel H. *To Sell Is Human: The Surprising Truth about Moving Others.* New York: Riverhead, 2012.

Selling Secrets That Work

Mullen, David J. *The Million-dollar Financial Advisor: Powerful Lessons and Proven Strategies from Top Producers.* New York: American Management Association, 2010.

Richardson, Linda. *Perfect Selling: Open the Door, Close the Deal.* New York: McGraw-Hill, 2008.

Behavioral Selling

Flaxington, Beverly D. *Understanding Other People: The Five Secrets to Human Behavior.* United States: ATA, 2010.

Rohm, Robert A. *Positive Personality Profiles: "d-i-s-c-over" Personality Insights to Understand Yourself—and Others!* Atlanta, GA: Personality Insights, 2000.

Rosenberg, Merrick, and Daniel Silvert. *Taking Flight!: Master the DISC Styles and Transform Your Career, Your Relationships—Your Life.* Upper Saddle River, NJ: FT, 2013.

Increasing Referrals

Maher, Michael J. *(7L): The Seven Levels of Communication.* Dallas, TX: BenBella, 2014.

Misner, Ivan R. *The World's Best-known Marketing Secret: Building Your Business with Word-of-mouth Marketing.* Austin, TX: Bard & Stephen, 1994.

Sernovitz, Andy. *Word of Mouth Marketing: How Smart Companies Get People Talking.* Chicago, IL: Kaplan Pub., 2006.

Centers of Influence (COI)

Maselli, Frank. *Referrals, The Professional Way: 10 Strategies for Networking with Top Clients & Centers of Influence.* Advantage Media Group, 2013.

Mullen, David J. *The Million-dollar Financial Advisor: Powerful Lessons and Proven Strategies from Top Producers.* New York: American Management Association, 2010.

Prince, Russ A., and Brett Van Bortel. "What Centers Of Influence Want." *Financial Advisor Magazine* (February 3, 2014).

Building a Sales Culture

Griego, Michael. *42 Rules to Increase Sales Effectiveness.* Cupertino, CA: Super Star, 2009.

Kasper, Jim. *Creating the #1 Sales Force: What It Takes to Transform Your Sales Culture.* Kaplan Business, 2005.

Effective Storytelling

Scott, David Meerman. *The New Rules of Sales and Service: How to Use Agile Selling, Real-time Customer Engagement, Big Data, Content, and Storytelling to Grow Your Business.* New York: Wiley, 2014.

West, Scott, and Mitch Anthony. *Storyselling for Financial Advisors: How Top Producers Sell.* Chicago: Dearborn, 2000.

Managing Time to Focus On Business Building

Drucker, David J., and Joel P. Bruckenstein. *Technology Tools for Today's High-margin Practice: How Client-centered Financial Advisors Can Cut Paperwork, Overhead, and Wasted Hours.* Hoboken, NJ: John Wiley & Sons, 2013.

Knapp, Rob. *The Supernova Advisor: Crossing the Invisible Bridge to Exceptional Client Service and Consistent Growth.* Hoboken, NJ: John Wiley & Sons, 2008.

Mullen, David J. *The Million-dollar Financial Advisor: Powerful Lessons and Proven Strategies from Top Producers.* New York:

American Management Association, 2010.

Ongoing Communication to Deepen Relationships

Green, Charles H. *Trust-based Selling: Using Customer Focus and Collaboration to Build Long-term Relationships*. New York: McGraw-Hill, 2006.

Maslansky, Michael. *The Language of Trust: Selling Ideas in a World of Skeptics*. New York: Prentice Hall, 2010.

Generational Selling: Crossing the Divide

Fromm, Jeff, and Christie Garton. *Marketing to Millennials: Reach the Largest and Most Influential Generation of Consumers Ever*. AMACOM, 2013.

Marston, Cam. *Generational Selling Tactics That Work: Quick and Dirty Secrets for Selling to Any Age Group*. Hoboken, NJ: John Wiley & Sons, 2011.

Taylor, Gabriela. *Targeting Your Market (Marketing across Generations, Cultures & Gender)*. CreateSpace, 2012.

Creating a Sales Program for the Next Generation

Espinoza, Chip, Mick Ukleja, and Craig Rusch. *Managing the Millennials: Discover the Core Competencies for Managing Today's Workforce*. Hoboken, NJ: John Wiley & Sons, 2010

Orrell, Lisa. *Millennials into Leadership: The Ultimate Guide for Gen Y's Aspiring to Be Effective, Respected, Young Leaders at Work*. Deadwood, Or.: Intelligent Women's Pub., 2009.

About the Author

As The Human Behavior Coach®, Be D. Flaxington has developed an expe in understanding people and their be ior and in teaching them how to "re others, connect with them quickly, communicate effectively. She has de oped several proprietary programs, including The S.H.I.F. Model, which focuses on understanding the human fact *The Six Keys to Confident Presenting,* which helps advisors understand their audience and present effectively; and *T Five Secrets to Successful Selling,* which uses human behavior its basis for selling to others.

Beverly has spent close to 30 years in the investment business and has been chief operating officer of a $2.5 billion advisory firm, where she developed the sales and marketing program. She is a Certified Hypnotherapist and has deep experience in helping others to make behavioral change happen.

She is a college professor and teaches at Suffolk University, where her trademarked programs are used with students to learn effective change management and problem-solving.

Beverly has worked with thousands of financial advisors, teaching them how to understand their own style of communicating, read others, and provide financial planning and wealth management in a truly consultative and behaviorally oriented way.